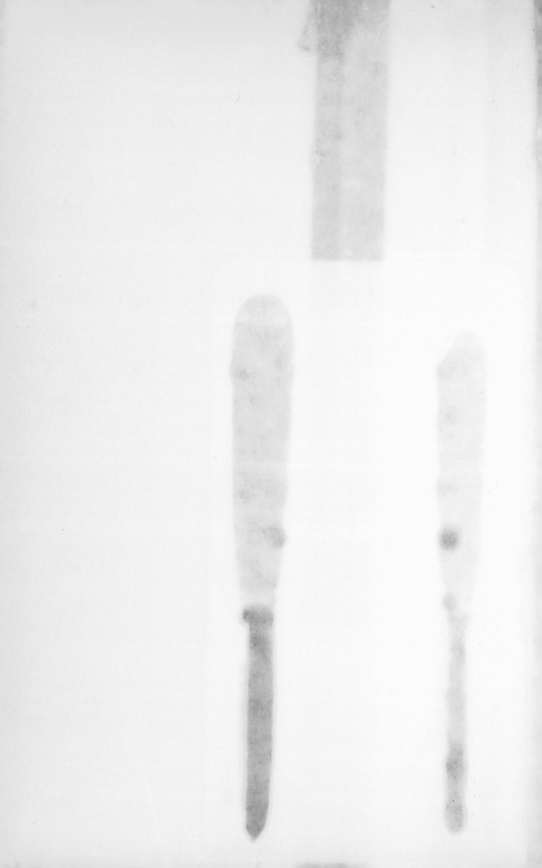

SKI WOMAN'S WAY

Elissa Slanger
and Dinah B. Witchel

SUMMIT BOOKS
New York

Published by *Summit Books*
A Simon & Schuster Division of Gulf & Western Corporation
Simon & Schuster Building
1230 Avenue of the Americas
New York, New York 10020

Designed by Stanley S. Drate

Manufactured in the United States of America

1   2   3   4   5   6   7   8   9   10

Library of Congress Cataloging in Publication Data

Slanger, Elissa.
  Ski Woman's Way.

  1. Skiing for women. 2. Woman's Way Ski Seminars
(Firm) I. Witchel, Dinah B., joint author. II. Title.
GV854.34.S54   796.9'3   79-19205

ISBN 0-671-40104-1

To LeRoy
who heard my voice and recognized me

and

To Larry
who is always in Cleveland when the boiler breaks,
who is always here when it matters

Contents

Foreword
Woman's Way: How It Began

It was a short article in a small California newspaper, describing a series of ski weeks for women only at Squaw Valley, California. The article brought more than 150 letters to Elissa Slanger's desk, letters which requested—sometimes demanded—times, dates, places for the next ski weeks.

The letters confirmed what Elissa already knew: that thousands of women want to learn to ski or to ski better, but are confused, fearful, tense, and intimidated by the mechanical, sometimes tyrannical way in which skiing is traditionally taught. That is why Woman's Way Ski Seminars were started.

The seminars began in the winter of 1976. Elissa, responding to comments from women who were making no progress in established ski schools, matched a group of women instructors with a small group of women students.

Elissa drew on her experience not only as a ski teacher, but as a student of Zen and an explorer in the jungle of sports learning theory and feminist literature. She planned a ski week that included hours on the snow; workshops on body awareness, equipment, and clothing; rap sessions on fear and on the woman's experience in skiing, including conceptions and misconceptions of the woman's role in sports; plus fondue parties, candlelit dinners, and wine and cheese picnics on the hill.

The experiment was so successful that it expanded within three years to twenty-three weeks of seminars at ten major ski areas from New Hampshire to California and is continuing to grow.

Scores of women have passed through the program, dozens have returned to repeat the experience, hundreds have tried to reserve space. Why? What makes this program more than a coffee klatch on skis?

First of all, it is at long last an acknowledgment that women skiers are different from men skiers. Although many women may take to skiing as if they were born on skis, many others struggle through learning to ski as if they were giving birth to the sport.

Actually, both men and women suffer from the way that sports are taught today. Even in skiing, usually regarded as an area for individualistic activity, the learning and teaching atmosphere is charged with competitiveness. The ski instructor is the model: "Look at me, follow me, see how well I ski; you will learn to ski this well." If you do not, you are a "failure."

Dangled in front of every would-be skier via movies, magazines, books, and brochures is the Perfect Skier, the one who skis the most difficult slopes at the highest speeds in fluid motion. It is for this impossible perfection that we should strive and if we do not achieve it, then we have failed, not only as skiers, but by implication, as persons.

Even the body-aware "new-consciousness" methods of teaching have the Perfect Skier as goal, although the goal is achieved far less painfully than through the still wide-spread "me teacher—you puppet" routines of learning.

What Woman's Way does is put the Perfect Skier in his place, which is at the bar of the base lodge regaling others with tales of his exploits. On the slopes now are the Real Skiers, imperfect, technically flawed, but able to involve themselves in the pleasure of the moment, the enjoyment of physical effort, the pride in meeting realistic self-determined challenges.

Essentially, Woman's Way says, "You choose how good a skier you want to be, your maximum level of involvement and pleasure—do not let someone else choose it for you."

The Woman's Way classes are humanistic and non-dogmatic, an attitude toward skiing rather than a method of teaching. Students and instructors meet each other as real people, exploring not only the pleasures of the mountain, but the psychological webs we spin, the physical differences between the sexes, and societal barriers. The learning process is viewed as being as enjoyable as the sport, and skiing at any level—beginner, intermediate, expert—as an opportunity for enrichment and personal insight.

This is an approach to learning skiing, and all sports, brought about by the needs of women, women unable to fit themselves into the "right" mold, the aggressive, fearless, fast male stereotype. Its implications for learning and enjoying skiing are much broader: a rejection of the "winning is everything" attitude that still permeates sport, a return to the idea of sport as "re-creation," a discovery of pleasure in movement and skill, of the creative forces nourished by skiing and all sports, and an opportunity to realize the harmony of mind and body which makes for almost unlimited personal growth.

Woman's Way, not incidentally, also produces good skiers.

Dinah Witchel had also been exploring and had written

about the problems women have in learning to ski. In New York City, she had come to many of the same conclusions that Elissa had in Squaw Valley. They met on a mountain in Colorado and this book is an outgrowth of that meeting.

We have both learned a lot as we have written the book. We have learned something about skiing and about how we learn, much about ourselves and our roles as women both on and off skis. We have had a lot of help.

Oh-oh, you say. Here come the acknowledgments. You're right, here they come. As readers we had wondered why authors bothered with the terse lists of people-without-whom-they-could-not-have-authored. As writers, now we know. We owe thanks, of course, to those experts who read the manuscript, made suggestions, whose brains we picked. But writing a book is an intense experience. To express our true feelings to those family members and friends who with extraordinary sensitivity encouraged, scolded, soothed, absorbed fits of temper, dragged us back into the real world from time to time, gave what they had to give and then let us alone, would take another book. So here is our terse list and we hope that those whom we thank will read volumes between the lines:

Most of all, the students and instructors of Woman's Way whose insights seem infinite and who never hesitate to share them or to dig deeper for clearer understanding; Mort Lund, contributing editor of *Ski* magazine and a member of the board of the Woman's Way program, whose own contribution to humanism in skiing is ground-breaking; Lyn Ballard, who shared her ideas, her views, and gave her unfailing emotional support; Pam Levesque, who in the pinch helped to handle the burden of Woman's Way, the program, so Elissa could work on *Woman's Way*, the book; John and Elisabeth Witchel and John and Alice Brown, the latter grandparents of the former who gave the idea of family back its good name; Rita Frank, Diane d'Almeida, Barbara Nelson, Doug Pfeiffer, Lito Tejada-

Flores, Denise Young; George Bauer and the staff of *Ski* magazine for their support of the Woman's Way program; Al Greenberg, John Auran, and the staff of *Skiing* magazine; John Brockman and Katinka Matson, our agents, and Chris Steinmetz, our editor.

SKI WOMAN'S WAY

1

Skiing: A Woman's View

This is a book about women and skiing.

Alpine skiing is like flying. To stand at the top of the world. To launch into space and plunge down fast or slow, in time with the music in your own mind, isolated by wind and cold, stimulated by the visual beauty, a little bit afraid, aware always of the risks but always in control. It is a richly fulfilling experience.

The rewards of the senses—the motion, the scenery, the slither of snow, flickering scent of pine and quiver of cold—are matched by the awareness of mastery. Not mastery of nature, but mastery of your own body, mastery of the skills necessary to get from the top of the mountain to the bottom with grace, elegance, safety. To stop when you want to stop, to choose your pace, to have a sense that you and the mountain are friends, are one.

There are apparently more than four million women who have tasted that experience. Some of them ski extraordinarily well, so well that among the Olympic and World Championship medals won by United States skiers, nineteen out of twenty-three were won by women.

Women not only fly on skis, they dance, flip, pirouette, earn a living, star in films and commercials, teach, learn, and simply have a good time.

If we, as women, ski so well, why do we need a book just for us?

Unfortunately skiing has not been quite so easy for most women. While many ski very well indeed, another great number, sadly, tried it and abandoned it. Or they ski only for the sake of husband and kids—stuck at a plateau, not really enjoying it.

Some women who ski think of themselves as "too timid." They feel overwhelmed, frustrated. No matter how they try they can't seem to get the hang of it. They feel "unteachable," inept, defeated. Some women have hung on grimly, determined to conquer the sport, but always feeling inadequate next to their male companions. Others settled for sticking to the easy slopes, where the humiliation factor is minimized.

The grimness and the pain, the sense of defeat, is unnecessary. Learning to ski can be as joyous an experience as flying off the top of a mountain, and it is an experience to which any woman has access.

Any woman can learn to ski. That many women who want to don't is not because there is something wrong with women. It's because there is still a good deal awry with society and skiing pedagogy. It is because skiing has been a man's world with teaching systems and skiing systems developed by men, for men's physiques, men's habits, men's attitudes.

The norm in skiing is the male experience. When we ski, we measure ourselves against a standard, a set of values that has been established by outsiders, by people who are not like us. Women come to skiing as strangers in a strange land. The Perfect Skier is one who is aggressive, strong, fast, and "attacks" the mountain—a man. The woman who comes closest to the standard of perfection is said to "ski like a man"—the ultimate compliment.

There is nothing wrong with being aggressive and strong, with skiing fast, with "attacking" the mountain. Nothing wrong with it for men and nothing wrong with it for women. But it is not the only possible way to ski. There is nothing wrong with "caressing" a mountain either, for example.

This is not to catalog our woes or to present women as victims and men as victimizers. Many men, too, suffer from the aggressive approach to skiing and to ski instruction. For men as well as for women there are alternatives; there is the opportunity to express in skiing, as in everything else, the person you are.

Women Are Different from Men ━━━━━━

To be a woman is wonderful. We are different from men. Our perceptions are different, our sense of ourselves and our relationships with the world are different, our values are different, our bodies are different, our growing up is different, our adult years and old age are different. We process and interpret information differently and our experience of sport is different.

Many of us still have only a nebulous sense of our own wonder, our own value. Because society still sets its standards by and places more value on the way men perform, women tend to bury or denigrate their sense of themselves.

We are very oriented in our world to Numero Uno, to the best: there must be a best diet, a best way to educate children, a best way to grow flowers, a best way to be your own best friend. There can be only one number one and if there are two sexes to choose between, then one must be better than the other. That is sad. To live only by the standards of better and best means we wall ourselves off from the richness of experience and experiment. Say there are two roads from your home to your summer vacation spot. They are very different roads. One is a super highway and fast; one is meandering and beautiful. Some days we want to go fast; some days we want to meander. One route is not better than the other, it is only different. Each has value and importance.

This is not to say that there is a total polarity between men and women, that the roads never converge. There is some of the male and male experience in women, some of the female and female experience in men. A whole and healthy person in a whole and healthy world has a balance of the two. In general, however, the female experience has been and is undervalued.

In the struggle of women to balance the scales, to achieve equal opportunity in jobs and politics and sports, there have been misunderstandings. Particularly in sports, as we sought to equalize opportunity, some equalized anatomy as well. That meant men and women were identical, that women in sports were potentially capable of meeting male standards in performance.

Therein lies the rub, of course. Standards set by men. There are physical differences between women and men and it is unlikely that women will ever be able to equal men's achievements in demanding physical sports. But it seems to us that this is beside the point. The gap between the physical potential of the sexes is indeed narrowing; many of what we considered inherent physical differences are proving to be in great part environmentally induced. Although this is interesting and important, we, as women, must be careful not to throw out the baby with the bathwater. In the process of finding out how much like men we really are, we must not lose sight of our own special abilities and qualities.

Women can bring to skiing a new dimension that can only enhance the experience for both sexes.

It is important for a woman (or a man) to set her own

standards of performance—to bring to skiing those things she does best, those values that mean the most to her, those qualities that best represent her. But in order to do that, we must try to understand not only what our value is as women, but the forces that distort the skiing experience for many women.

Let us discuss the differences between women and men and how these differences relate to skiing. We can look at some of the physiological and psychological reasons "why a woman can't be more like a man"—why her skiing and approach to skiing are different.

The Physiological Differences

Folklore has it that men are strong, noble, intelligent, creative, brave, analytical, and adventurous. Women are timid, emotional, frail, intuitive, and full of moral turpitude. A book called *The Longest War* points out that a favored view of women in the past has been that "the best of woman is but a lesser man." Aristotle even had it that men were so superior to women that men had more teeth.

Science put that canard to rest, but even among scientists stereotypes die hard. At the turn of the century, when scientists were doing research on the functions of the parts of the brain, they put forth a theory that the frontal lobes of the brain were the seat of intelligence. It was then reported that although the parietal lobes of the brain were larger in females than males, the frontal lobes of women were smaller than those of men. That confirmed that females were dumber than men, that they were "but lesser men."

Later some scientists advanced a new theory that the parietal lobes were the organs of intellect. Researchers scrambled back to their anatomical laboratories and rushed to report that parietal lobes were smaller in women than in men and that women's frontal lobes were larger. So much for the objectivity of science.

Research in recent years, particularly since women have begun both to do the experiments and monitor the reports, has been much more successful in eliminating obvious sexist biases. As it stands now, the existence of some physiological differences are almost universally agreed upon; others, long believed in, are now disputed.

It is generally agreed that up to the age of puberty there is very little difference between boys and girls either in strength, endurance, or agility because of their sex.

After puberty:

• Women begin to secrete estrogens, develop breasts, and begin a menstrual cycle; their hips become fuller. Men secrete androgens, develop proportionally more muscle in their chest and shoulders and arms and grow taller than women. The proportion of the body that is muscle tissue is greater in men than in women.

• Women have more fat as a percentage of body weight than do men. This is an advantage in endurance sports, such as marathon running and cross-country skiing. The fuel (it is called glycogen) stored in muscle tissue is depleted after a period of activity and the muscles must then call on the glycogen stored in fat. Women, one might say, have more storage tanks.

• Women have a greater proportion of long-fiber muscles, men a greater proportion of short-fiber muscles. Long-fiber muscles are endurance muscles, short-fiber muscles are explosive power muscles. Women thus have the potential to do relatively better on long cross-country treks than on mogul-bashing.

• Women also seem to have lighter bones than men but it now appears that this may not be genetic, but a function of lack of exercise. Exercise stimulates bone growth as well as muscle development and slows the loss of minerals which help bones to become strong and dense.

• Because of their larger size, men have more red blood

corpuscles and are thus able to take up more iron. Iron is necessary for the blood to carry oxygen; therefore men may be able to carry and utilize larger quantities of oxygen more efficiently than women. Also iron lost during menstruation may not be replaced quickly, affecting women's oxygen-carrying capacity.

☆ • Two anatomical differences that usually affect the way a woman skis are her wider pelvis and her more elastic body tissue. The wider pelvis is the distinctive anatomical difference between the male and the female skeleton. There are those extreme unisexists who say you cannot tell the difference between a male and a female skeleton. But anyone who reads crime reports and detective novels with regularity knows that the lowliest county sheriff can detect the difference between a male and female skeleton buried in the woods. Because the pelvis is wider, the angle at which the femur or long thighbone joins the pelvis is different in men and women. This affects the way a woman stands and moves. Also, women do seem to have more elastic body tissue, including joints and ligaments, making them more flexible (it is usually easier for a woman to touch her toes or do a split than it is for a man). This difference will affect the way she edges her skis.

• A woman's body mass is distributed differently. That is, given a man and woman of equal weight, a woman will have a greater proportion of that weight around the pelvis, abdomen, and thigh than will a man. This makes a slight difference in center of gravity.

The ways these anatomical differences affect a woman's skiing will be discussed in more detail in Chapter 8 (Ski Tips for Women Only).

These are the basic physiological differences between women and men that are pertinent to skiing. It is important to know there are real differences so that we do not create new myths that Eve is but Adam with a uterus. It is more important to know which differences are real and which are not so that we do not perpetuate the old myths that women are frail and physically incompetent, so that we give the next generation and the generation after a chance to realize their physical potential.

We See Ourselves as Society Sees Us ━━━━

We are strongly affected by how others view us and how we view ourselves. If we are thought of as "frail," as incapable of exertion, we will conform to that image in varying degrees. And old images, old stereotypes, are hard to shake.

They are insidious and we perpetuate them without knowing it. Take the idea that women are fragile, dependent creatures. Females do not start out life as fragile infants. It appears that if anything females are actually healthier than male children, less susceptible to disease. But girl children are perceived as fragile and are cuddled and held more than male infants after about three months. That cuddling—and the psychological cuddling that continues when the girl is older—creates dependence, particularly if contrasted with males who are pushed out of the parental arms much earlier.

While cuddling is pleasurable, very pleasurable, it also raises the question, "If I am being cuddled and they (the males) are not, there must be something different about me. I must need cuddling more because I need to be protected more."

At school, the stereotypes are reinforced again, sometimes unconsciously. A study of sex stereotypes in children's readers showed constant reference to girls as helpless, boys as competent and adventurous.

"My Sally has fallen into the water," the little girl tells Dick. "Can't you save her?"

"Oh, Raymond, boys are much braver than girls."

These are lines from children's stories today, not in Victorian times. Even girls who have been encouraged to be adventurous will read this and note, "Oh, that is how girls should act." In gym class, when less is demanded of a girl than of a boy, it reinforces the idea that women are more frail, less capable, in need of protection.

For example, although there is little disagreement that up to the age of puberty virtually no difference between boys and girls exists in terms of strength, agility, or endurance, the revised (1976) standards handed down to elementary schools by the American Alliance of Health, Physical Education and Recreation sharply differ in standards set for prepubescent boys and girls. Nine- and ten-year old boys are expected to complete a 50-yard dash in 8.2 seconds, nine- and ten-year old girls in 8.6 seconds; boys to jump 4 feet 11 inches from a standing start, girls 4 feet 8 inches; boys to do 31 flexed leg sit-ups in 60 seconds, girls only 27 sit-ups. Boys are asked to chin themselves on a bar only once; girls are not even expected to be able to do that—they are required to hang from a bar, arms flexed, for 9 seconds.

As children grow older, the standards for boys and girls grow farther and farther apart. Surely if less is expected of us as girls when there are no real physical differences, we will give less. More important, we will come to truly believe that we are capable of less.

While parents and even schools are paying lip service to the notion that men and women are equal—and indeed may believe it—these other messages are also being transmitted to girls and boys. This kind of conditioning continues through childhood and accelerates in adolescence when the physical differences separate the sexes even more.

While it is important to learn and to know which differences are inherent and which are not, nevertheless, for us as grown women approaching a sport like skiing, it is a moot point. The fact is that our bones *are* smaller and smaller bones break more easily. The fact is that our soft tissue—muscles, ligaments, tendons—aren't as well developed, perhaps are even semiatrophied in some of us.

Recently, Elissa, at a ski industry convention, was assigned to a room with a woman who, although she worked in the ski industry, did not ski much. She had spent so much of her teen and adult life in high-heeled shoes that she had to walk on the balls of her feet when she was barefoot. She hadn't been born with severely shortened Achilles tendons, but she had developed them nevertheless. This would surely affect her ability to ski.

Physical differences, genetic or induced by shoe designers, don't mean that women can't learn to ski very well, even wonderfully. But they do indicate that most women cannot—and do not—ski like a man.

As one of the Woman's Way instructors said, "When I see a man do something difficult in skiing, I don't automatically assume that I can do the same thing."

But because skiing is one of the very few vigorous sports where men and women participate together, in a sense compete with each other, it is easy to choose a male as model. But trying to ski like a man can be frustrating for a woman and even frightening. She can seem "cautious," "unaggressive," "emotional" by comparison. If she skis like a woman, she will find her own style, her own pace without frustration or fear.

How High Can We Jump?

Besides the actual physical differences between women and men, one of the most important factors affecting a woman's approach to skiing is that she does not know her physical limitations and capabilities as well as a man does. Little boys are always testing themselves—how high they can jump, how much they can carry. This continues through their adolescence. Even a little girl who is considered a tomboy as a child usually becomes less physical in her teens. Peer pressure, societal stereotypes, a long list of factors are brought to bear. The result is that a woman enters adulthood—and comes to skiing—with much less idea of her physical capabilities and limitations than the average man has. It is thus no wonder that she seems "overcautious." She is not sure what it is she can and cannot do. She needs time and space to get to know her body better, to learn her potential, to build her confidence. To be thought of as timid is painful. The woman in her effort to please (we are notorious pleasers) may push herself beyond where she feels comfortable or may give up. Skiing, under these circumstances, will very soon cease to be fun.

And lest you think the situation is changing dramatically with today's children, that the passage of equality in sports-funding legislation, the surfacing in the public eye of attractive and active women like Billie Jean King and Virginia Wade have wiped out all the years of white gloves and girdles that went before, look around more carefully.

Recently, Elissa spent an afternoon with her neighbors in California, an unusually active family, even for California, and a family in which the women in particular are viewed by others and view themselves as talented athletes. There are two teenaged children, a boy about thirteen, a girl about fifteen. The girl swims, plays tennis, skis; she is at first glance a new woman. They sat by the pool, the girl and the adults. The girl went for a swim, then she sunned and joined the socializing. Her brother spent the entire afternoon perfecting a leap onto a Styrofoam board in the pool. By the end of the afternoon he could land on it and balance for several seconds. The men in the group were intrigued. They got up and tried it themselves; the women did not.

Right there, Elissa thought, is where it starts.

Another day, another neighbor. This one with younger children, about six and eight. Friends were visiting. The boys spent the afternoon running and chasing; the girls played tea party. There is nothing wrong with playing tea party; there is nothing wrong with roughhousing. What is askew is that roughhousing is still encouraged in boys and not in girls; that tea parties are encouraged for girls but not for boys. If it appears that these phenomena are only true among Elissa's friends and that we are overly sensitive to them, take a look at the December 4, 1978, issue of *Newsweek* magazine, which reported on the burgeoning sport of peewee football. Here little five- and six-year-old boys dress up in helmet, shoulder pads, and mouth guards and play block and tackle in preparation for their midget superbowl. On the sidelines, little five- and six-year-old girls dress up in short red skirts and vests and wave red and white pom-poms in the air practicing for life roles as cheerleaders to their men. As one observer said, "It is obscene."

If part of a woman's hesitancy in learning to ski comes from a lack of experience in sports, another part may come from her lack of motivation. One way in which males traditionally prove themselves is through physical prowess. Women do not have to be athletic to prove they are women. On the one hand this is good—it gives the woman more freedom to admit to fear, and, by admitting to it, deal with it. A man might not even admit the fear to himself—it would be too damaging to his self-image. On the other hand, the woman would be more likely to succumb to the fear, more readily allow herself to be cautious. She probably would not have as much motivation to push herself. If she were uncomfortable she might give up. If she were frightened she might quit. If she were hurt she might not challenge herself again.

Is Skiing Unfeminine?

Much of what is asked of a woman in a sports situation runs counter to her societal stereotype, to what society expects of her and what she has come to expect of herself.

Our culture views aggression in a man as a positive characteristic implying strong character, virility, leadership. Aggression in a woman is seen as castrating, bossy, tough, "unfeminine." A girl, without realizing it, internalizes society's messages. She enters a sport situation, she starts to ski and is told to be more aggressive. A real conflict may arise. She may not know how to be aggressive. She may feel uncomfortable being aggressive. It is not so easy to override lifetime taboos.

One of the problems that coaches of girls encounter is the battles their athletes must wage against the stigmas of society, stigmas caused by societal stereotypes. These competitive athletes are dealing, in spades, with some of the prejudices even recreational athletes come up against: that a woman who excels in sports is a "jock" and will develop big bulging muscles which men won't like.

In the April 1979 issue of *Womensports*, Anna Quindlin reports, "On a recent night I was running by the World Trade Center . . . when a paunchy postal worker hovering in a doorway called out, 'Hey, toots. Looking good.'

" 'How far can you run, fatso?' I called back, as the man's co-workers chortled over his discomfort.

"But as I pulled away, picking up some speed, I heard him say, 'With those muscles you'll never get a man.' "

There is a lot in those paragraphs—the outrageous condescension of the man (he may have thought he was even being flattering—a harmless attempt at flirtation), the obvious rage of the woman, her hostile comeback. No wonder there is so much anger and resentment on both sides in this age of change.

The article from which this is quoted is called "The Intimidation Factor: It Can Be a Woman's Greatest Opponent." It details anecdote after anecdote about girls and women, who, athletically competent and confident on their own or with other women, fell apart when competing with men. The author brings up possible explanations: Woman's fear of success. An ingrained belief that men deserve to win. A traditional "massaging" of the male ego. A little voice that we have carried around in our head since girlhood that says "you can't do that." The fact that men—and our whole society perhaps—don't take a woman's athletic attempts seriously.

A few years back, before she started Woman's Way, Elissa was giving a private skiing lesson to a couple. They were both beginners. The woman was quite talented physically, although she hadn't been aware of it. She was catching on to skiing more quickly than was her husband. She was delighted with her newfound skills. As the lesson continued, her husband became increasingly sullen and sarcastic. Tension developed between them. Suddenly, before Elissa's eyes and within a matter of moments, the scene changed. The woman became awkward. She couldn't get the hang of it. And her husband—her husband became solicitous, protective. The marital crisis was averted. We cannot put all the blame on the husband in this tableau. Without the tacit agreement of the wife the stereotyped relationship would not be, could not stay as it was. It was a complicity between the two of them.

Many of us have overcome, are overcoming, the limitations of these stereotypes, but almost every woman will recognize herself in what Barnard College president Matina Horner once said: "The most highly competent and otherwise achievement-motivated young women, when faced with a conflict between their feminine image and expressing their competencies or developing their abilities and interests, adjust their behaviors to their internalized sex role stereotypes."

In other words, if a woman has a choice between appearing competent and appearing "feminine," she will come down on the side of "femininity."

In the mid-seventies, Elissa was an examiner for instructor certification. At one exam a very young, attractive woman instructor came before the examining board. She was being tested for the first level of certification. Despite her age, she seemed competent and relatively confident. But not for long. Other than Elissa, the members of the examining board were men. They began playfully teasing the young woman. Before Elissa's eyes, the instructor's confidence crumbled, her air of professionalism dissipated. She became what she was being treated as, an attractive girl, to be flirted with, but not to be taken seriously. After she had left the room, Elissa pointed out to the board what had happened. They were shocked. All they had meant to do was set the young woman at ease, to make her feel more relaxed.

Part of growing up a woman also means avoiding physical exertion. Men perspire and ladies glow, as the old saying goes. Huffing and puffing and staining your gym clothes with sweat is not ladylike. The thousands of women who have taken up running are changing this for many of us. They have come to understand that the rewards of physical exertion, the sense of total well-being, far outweigh any residual distaste for sweat-soaked hair or the effort involved in getting started. Men grow up understanding this and also understanding that the routine consequences of physical exertion may be, at the least, sore muscles.

But "women have always been so shielded from body injury and risk of pain that most women experience anxiety during physical activity that might result in body contact or roughness," say Patsy Neal and Thomas Tutko in *Coaching Girls and Women*.

That certainly includes skiing in which falling is part of

the beginner's routine. Nobody, male or female, welcomes bodily injury or pain. But a bruise is only a bruise; a stiff muscle is only a stiff muscle. It is when it takes on emotional significance that it becomes a barrier.

One of our Woman's Way instructors remembers a time around puberty when she was playing touch football with her brothers, as she had done throughout her childhood. Her father called her aside.

"You will have to start being a little more careful, now," he said to her. "You are getting to be a young lady. You can hurt yourself."

She can still remember her resentment—and her alarm. She was not yet very sure what being a woman entailed. She was going through that period when her body seemed almost foreign to her. How would she hurt it, she wondered? It must have something to do with being a woman.

Neal and Tutko continue: "The problem is intensified by the emphasis that has been placed on the attractive physical appearance of the girl or woman. Any girl or woman who feels her looks are vital to her popularity avoids activity that might blemish her appearance."

Scabs and bruises blemish appearance. Hair that is flattened out by a ski hat or is wet and bedraggled diminishes attractiveness. To some women this doesn't seem so important, but to others the chance of breaking a nail is a deterrent to exertion. Probably we all are sensitive to the conflict to some degree differing only in how much we have invested in looking our absolute best, in the degree to which we feel our survival in the marketplace depends on it.

Fear of success, fear of seeming masculine, fear of not looking attractive, fear of "showing up" a man, fear of hurting ourselves. What do we do about all of this? Well, first of all we recognize that these fears exist. Just the knowledge that we are not alone, that others feel as we do, that there are reasons for our insecurities is reassuring. We cannot begin to change these things in ourselves until we recognize them. From that identification and self-knowledge, a sense of who we are and what we want—not what someone else wants for us—can develop.

Then we will feel as Elissa's friend Randa did, when she was skiing at Squaw Valley. A man skied up behind her and said, "You ski just like a woman."

"Thank you," said Randa.

2

What Skiing Can Do for Women (and What Women Can Do for Skiing)

For people who love skiing as we do, it is tempting to say that skiing will change your life. It will make you brave, wise, reverent, thrifty, and give you a suntan in winter. We can guarantee the tan. Whether skiing will change you in any of the other ways or whether such changes would be desirable in your life is a very personal matter.

If you want to change your life, then maybe skiing is a tool which can help you do it. But you can also change your life by becoming a nun, joining the Peace Corps, or having a baby, all more radical and probably less expensive than taking up skiing.

It is important to keep sport in perspective. Because women have for so many centuries been shorted on an aspect of life which confers such important social, physical, and psychological benefits, it is likely that the pendulum may swing the other way, that women may invest in sport as the solution to life's inequities and puzzlements. It is not the solution, but it can be much more than keeping fit.

When women are asked why they ski, the answers are

usually something such as it's fun, it's an activity to share with family or friends, it's outdoors, it's exercise. A sport shouldn't really be asked to give much more than that, but skiing can.

One of the things that skiing can do is help a woman or a man break out of those stereotypes we spoke of in the previous chapter. Women who accept the male way of doing things as the right way—in sports or in anything else—and want only to prove that they are as good as men, that they can do anything men can do, are only trading one set of limits for another.

The degree to which people fit themselves into a stereotype, be it female or male, is the degree of their limitation. We all have the potential for all modes of behavior within us—for femaleness, for maleness, for ambiguity; for aggression, for pacifism; for intellectualism, for athleticism. The fewer of these attributes we express, the less full and rich our experience.

Skiing brings into focus those limits we set on ourselves—perfectionism, fear of success, fear of failure, lack of self-confidence, whatever they may be. Like most games and sports, skiing is a model of life or parts of life, a miniature of what George Leonard in *The Ultimate Athlete* calls the Game of Games.

But unlike everyday life, sport is a controlled environment. Like a child in a playground safely contained by a fence, an adult can explore her controlled environment, experimenting with different movements and different roles, different aspects of herself, without danger of major repercussions.

Specialists in child development agree that play and fantasy are the ways in which children explore and master not only their environment but themselves and their relationships with their peers and family. Unfortunately adults, especially women, begin to abandon play at puberty. They put away the things of a child too quickly.

To take our exploration to a mountain and play on skis

is to give ourselves an opportunity to practice and express types of behavior that have been suppressed or undeveloped in us. Men, for instance, caught in the trap of being aggressive, authoritarian, and unemotional, find an ideal opportunity in skiing to practice sensitivity to beauty, delicate, elegant movement, and gentle companionship.

In Woman's Way classes we experiment with aggressiveness. We play at being very unaggressive, we play at being as aggressive as we can. We play in between. We see how it feels to be timid, to be aggressive; we decide where we feel comfortable, where we feel uncomfortable. The idea is not to become more aggressive. The idea is to experience and express the full spectrum so that we are not limited by old habits and an old self-image.

Another game is role playing. Like actresses, we assume role after role, acting out the different parts of ourselves—the confident skier, the "happy-go-lucky" skier, the "show-off." We see that we can slip in and out of roles easily, that indeed our usual way of skiing (of being) is only another role.

Skiing, like almost all sports, intensifies and clarifies experience and perception. It is a means of confronting ourselves and our temperaments, our personalities and our self-images. And, if we want, of making changes. We can learn to set realistic goals for ourselves and to appreciate ourselves when we reach them. We can learn to enjoy our learning process—the sensations, the satisfactions, the growth. Time after time, in seminar after seminar, women express this in one way or another. "Now that I know I am capable of learning after all," said Gloria, "I can take up anything I want—scuba diving, flying, foreign languages."

As one woman instructor said, "My skis are my wings and I'm playing with them."

We can, on the ski slope, establish our personal limits, physical and psychological, experiment with them, test them. You may find, for instance, that you have the attribute of persistence, that you keep trying even if you fail again and again. You also find, however, that you are inflexible in your persistence; that you keep beating on the same door until it opens or your knuckles are sore. Now is the opportunity to change that.

For instance, you have been having trouble keeping pressure on the outside ski. You are getting frustrated, but you are stubborn. You keep trying with every turn to put more pressure on that ski. Try another door. Ease up, back off, and instead of trying to get pressure on that outside ski, take the pressure off the inside ski. Lift the tail of that ski off the snow. It serves the same purpose; if the weight is not on one ski it must be on the other.

Or you keep berating yourself because your weight on your skis is not where you think it should be. You try again and again, doggedly, to get forward as you were once told. How about giving yourself the freedom to experiment: Try putting your weight on various parts of the ski—farther back, way far forward, in the middle, rocking from place to place, zeroing in on what feels best for you.

"Come along with us to the Headwall," say your friends. "You should be challenging yourself more." You had been feeling comfortable, as if you were challenging yourself quite enough. But now you are in conflict. Flattered that they have invited you. Anxious to please them. Feeling the imperative of that "should." Whereas before you might have grimly acquiesced, this time you take stock and listen to your own inner voice.

"No, thank you," you say firmly. "This feels like my pace right now."

You are repatterning your behavior and testing yourself, your limits, your temperamental mechanisms in what is fundamentally a nonthreatening situation (it is nonthreatening in the sense that an embarrassing or "wrong" response will not cost you your job or your scholarship or a lover). You are rehearsing potential changes in other aspects of your life. You are learning to take responsibility for your own behavior.

Body and Soul Together ━━━━━━━━━━━

If you can learn much about yourself in skiing, you can learn even more about your body. Part of the pleasure of skiing is the joy of physical self-expression and control, the satisfaction of movement and skill. It is important for women, particularly, to become acquainted or reacquainted with their bodies as wonderful, complicated mechanisms.

Bodies are not just suitcases for the soul, not just objects to be decorated and kept slim. There is a great sense of physical well-being which comes from a day of physical exertion, the good fatigue of muscles well and happily used.

Sports also help women learn to deal realistically with physical discomfort and even pain. Athletes, for instance, have a much easier time in childbirth than do women who have no athletic background. They also need cesarean deliveries significantly less frequently.

Healthy bodies do nourish healthy minds—the Roman was right.

As runner Dr. George Sheehan says, do not undervalue the close relationship between body and soul; one affects the other. Physical activity is one way of handling psychological stress. It lets the body work off the anxieties and leaves you in a stronger psychological state to deal with emotional problems.

When you are skiing, for instance, it is very difficult to hold on to concerns and worries. You must be absorbed in the challenge of the sport. Lack of attention for a moment can result in crossed tips and a swan dive into the snow, so the cares of daily life are pushed aside. After a couple of hours on the mountain, if your concerns have not disappeared altogether, they come to mind in a new perspective.

Psychologists find that exercise produces greater emotional stability, less anxiety, greater self-assurance. To this list Dr. L. E. Trachtmann of Purdue adds more imagination and more "psychological courage." Another researcher, Dr. Arnold Mandell of the University of California, a psychiatrist who has successfully added exercise to the regimen of some of his patients, has found that those who are physically fit or attempting to be physically fit seem "to be more assertive, to exercise their dominant feelings more freely, and to show their aggressions more readily," in positive ways designed to further their life goals.

We are not yet sure why this is so. Some of these psychological benefits seem to be directly related to chemical changes in the body. Vigorous exercise, such as skiing, seems to encourage the release and the more effective utilization of substances in the body that literally affect the way we look at life. Whether through chemistry or simply because skiing away from it all is good therapy, playing hard does have the effect of relieving the kinds of stress caused by emotional tension and boredom. Apparently those who include active recreation in their lives are simply "happier" people.

In a survey conducted among men and women between thirty and seventy by John C. Flanagan of the American Institutes for Research, people were asked how satisfied they were with "the quality of life." Those most satisfied with their lives, given financial security and adequate health care, were those who included active recreation high on their lists of interests. In fact, the importance of active recreation—what Flanagan called the "biggest surprise"—rated above learning, creative expression, close friends, social life, children, relatives, community activity, and a close relationship with a spouse.

And skiing ranks among the top five of most desirable forms of recreation.

It is interesting to speculate on why active recreation is so important. Once the basic needs of life are satisfied—food, shelter, companionship—there is perhaps in all of us a need for challenge, an impetus toward growth. We yearn not only for self-awareness, but for self-improvement and self-realization. We Americans have expressed that in various ways in our history: the push to the last frontier, the push to improve technology, the push to achieve better standards of living, and now the push of the so-called Me Decade to explore ourselves. The drive to move on seems very deep in us. Perhaps sports such as skiing are so satisfying because they allow us to satisfy that drive quickly and easily. The challenges are clearcut, the growth is evident. The slope which you could not ski last winter you can ski this winter; the ice which terrified you last week, this week seems only a difficult piece of terrain.

Skiing has the added benefit of being a "risk" sport. Danger, real physical danger, is an element that is missing for most of us. There is a theory advanced by the distinguished scientist Dr. Sol Roy Rosenthal of the University of Illinois that risk sport is a basic need in mankind—and that includes womankind. Rosenthal speculates that man evolved to his present form by facing risks, daily risks from the elements, from animals, from other human beings. As natural risk subsided, man invented sports. But in our state of so-called advanced civilization even risk sports are becoming obsolescent, enjoyed second hand. We watch football games on television, rather than at the stadium, where at least we would be cold and uncomfortable and could identify with the participant on the field.

Says Rosenthal, "Risk exercise is not only a basic evolutionary need, but it gives exquisite joy and vigor. It also helps us maintain our sense of humor and perspective and, on the evidence I have found, a risk sport appreciably improves the participant's sex life."

One of our Woman's Way instructors told of her experiences kayacking in white water. It terrified her and she has chosen not to do it again. However, the one thing she liked about it was the way she felt afterward, when she was back on shore. Life seemed so beautiful. She saw the world around her with such clarity, she felt so calm, so peaceful.

With serenity and good sex as possible rewards, is it any wonder that risk sports like kayacking, surfing, and delta-wing kite flying have enjoyed such booms. So has skiing.

Stretching Your Senses ━━━━━━━━━━

All of us get caught every day in the web of trivia that marks our individual lives—getting up, going to work, finishing the assignment, the billing, the letter, getting to the meeting, the cleaners, the bank. More than almost any other activity, sport breaks into that routine, abruptly and thoroughly, providing an opportunity to refocus and readjust perspective. Some sports such as skiing offer more of an opportunity than others to extend ourselves beyond the mundane.

Skiing provides an opportunity to develop a relationship with the natural universe.

Says George Leonard, "Downhill skiing, perhaps more than any other sport, joins the geometric with the sensuous. Few moments in sport compare with that pause at the summit preceding a long delirous fall that will leave its tracks in the snow—the curves of human skill and desire."

Says no less a philosopher than Jean-Paul Sartre, "To ski . . . is to enable me to possess this field of snow . . . by my very course and activity as a skier, I am changing the matter and meaning of the snow."

To act upon the snow, to leave your tracks upon it, however, is to establish a relationship between you and the snow, to take the snow into your own experience and in a sense become one with it.

At high moments in skiing, you can lose the feeling of a self set apart from your surroundings, sometimes even lose the feeling of self altogether.

Elissa said in an interview with *Ski* magazine contributing editor Morten Lund: "What always fascinated me about skiing was the relation of it to the mind—what happens in the mind . . . it's that 'loss of duality,' the duality in which you are here and the rest of the world is out there. . . . Zen monastic life is built not only around sitting meditation, but around 'moving meditation' as well, meditating—that is, being totally aware—while walking, while gardening, while doing all the everyday motions.

The goal is to do these things with an appropriateness and attention that marks someone completely at one with the world. . . . I found that while years of [Zen] discipline enabled me to achieve an aware state in everyday things, it could happen spontaneously in skiing. Suddenly you were one with the mountain and snow and slopes."

For those who are reluctant, skeptical or shy about entering into the realm of the spiritually esoteric, skiing is a happy introduction to some of the rewards of "mysticism" without doing all the work.

For instance, skiing opens up awareness, provides an opportunity for "seeing reality with new eyes." One of the ways it does this is by forcing concentration, providing a focus for conscious concentration. Some meditation exercises, for instance, suggest that the student select an object outside herself, or a sound, or even one of her own bodily processes—breathing, heartbeat. Concentrate on that as much as possible to the exclusion of all else. When you finish the meditation—break the concentration—your perceptions are freshened and revived.

To some extent, the concentration demanded by skiing can provide that "meditative" focus. You are forced to "get into" what you are doing here and now, on this slope at this moment, or risk a fall. Narrowing your focus even more—by concentrating on how your ski edges feel on the snow, on the rhythm of your body, on the sound or feel of the snow—can make the meditative aspect even more effective. The ultimate reward is the "peak experience": all senses become more acute—data comes in purely and directly without filters and the body acts spontaneously in response. The feeling is sublime and you return to common reality feeling very relaxed, very calm, everything looks and sounds fresh, new.

You also return with a new respect for yourself. An awe at your unsuspected abilities. A sense of trust in your inner self, your body, which frees it from the need for constant conscious control and direction.

In *The Ultimate Athlete*, British golfer Tony Jacklin describes the "cocoon of concentration" he sometimes finds himself in: "When I'm in this state, this cocoon of concentration, I'm living *fully* in the present, not moving out of it . . . I'm aware of every half inch of my swing . . . I'm absolutely engaged, *involved* in what I'm doing at that particular moment. That's the important thing. That's the difficult state to arrive at. It comes and it goes . . ."

Highly trained athletes often report a "sports high," a moment or even a lengthy period of time during a game or a prolonged athletic experience in which their perceptions are radically altered. Michael Murphy and Rhea White cite many examples in *The Psychic Side of Sports*. The athletes, ranging from football players to tennis and golf players, use words like elation, exhilaration, rapture, euphoria to describe a state that seems to begin with acute awareness. Vision sharpens, hearing becomes more acute, even touch and taste are more sensitive. For some, the perception of time is altered—it moves faster or slower. Some get a surge of new energy which has been described as tapping an unknown energy source, like plugging into the cosmos.

Some of this has to do with the physical reactions and changes in body chemistry caused by the spectacular exertion of competitive athletes. But much of it has to do with the abandonment of prosaic modes of thought and the concentration on the matter at hand—blocking the tackle, hitting the ball, turning the skis. The blocking of extraneous data permits the data that is perceived to be experienced fully. Professional tasters, for instance, put away smoking, alcohol, and spicy foods so their taste buds will not be dulled when it's time to savor wine or tea or strawberry jam. It may also in some way permit us to process the information we are receiving in new ways; breaking up the old patterns of perception, the old nerve pathways, may permit new pathways to come into play which let us know other aspects of ourselves.

This "new perception" is carried to the extreme in marathon athletes, runners and swimmers particularly. Swimmer Diana Nyad reports extraordinary (and sometimes terrifying) hallucinations when she has been in the water for a number of hours. Of course, unlike runners or any other athlete, swimmers are left with few sensory reference points. Once the body is attuned to the temperature of the water and the rhythm of the stroke, there is little change in visual, auditory, or other sensory input. Nyad's altered state of consciousness may be beyond what you would care to experience.

Even those of us who are not athletes have these kinds of experiences in our lives in one form or another. We often don't recognize them for what they are, because they do not manifest themselves dramatically in hallucinations or "time slowing down." But we have all, one early morning, walked out of our still dim and gloomy homes into a day where the sun is just over the horizon and the air is clear and cool. We stop for a moment and hear the birds, see how green the leaves are, smell the greenness and the coolness, perhaps even sort out a hint of early flowers, feel the air on our skins brushing away the night. The moment passes and we move on thinking, What a beautiful morning. But just for an instant we have perceived it all as new and felt a part of it, as if the sun and the trees and the air were greeting us as we were greeting them.

Some of us—many of us probably—have felt that unity sometimes as we ski, the moment when the skier and the mountain, the snow and the sky are one, moving in one perfect rhythm. Those moments are to be treasured, to be recaptured and extended if possible. And we can also bring those fresh perceptions back to our real, sometimes troubled lives.

If these things seem to offer more than you want from skiing, if you don't want re-creation, but simple recreation, there's that too.

If a day of skiing does nothing else, it offers hours of simple pleasure. That's a very important aspect of sport, and one which we are likely to forget. When various dictionaries define sport, they define it in terms of its roots—to disport, to pleasure oneself. If all you bring back from a day or an hour of skiing is simply feeling good, that is enough. As one casual runner said when asked to probe her motives for running, "I just do it because it makes me feel wonderful and makes me feel competent."

Said another runner, "It's a celebration of life . . ."

We can discover that celebration of life in skiing. But to do that we have to take ourselves seriously as skiers.

The Other Side of Skiing

If we accept the premise that everything in life has its opposite—that there is no right hand without a left hand, no night without day, no Yin without Yang, no masculine without feminine—then it is appropriate to look also for the other side of skiing.

Because women are not programmed to the aggressive mode they often feel themselves to be second best on the slopes, no matter how well they ski. Because they are uncomfortable with viewing the mountain as the enemy, they feel a lack in them when the lack is really in the sport.

That's good. Not good that we feel ourselves deficient, but good that we are unfamiliar and uncomfortable with the socialization which suggests that skiing—or any sport—is a war game, that moguls are a mine field to be destroyed. It is good that we do not have to unlearn the rules of battle.

Because women have not been indoctrinated to sports the way that men have, they can be more open to alternative ways of viewing and approaching skiing. Traditional indoctrination includes concepts such as the one summed up by Vince Lombardi's now famous statement, "Winning isn't everything, it's the only thing." (Or as a ski coach expressed it, "Winning isn't everything, but coming in second is nothing.") If the winner, or the best, is "the only thing" and all else is "nothing," that doesn't leave much room for the appreciation of personal experience.

"Research and training for coaches and physical education instructors focuses tightly on performance at the expense of experience. Instructors ask how many times a boy or girl can chin, but not how it feels to chin, how it 'is,' " says George Leonard.

That most women haven't had as much athletic training as men makes it potentially easier for them to break out of the performance orientation. It makes it easier to put the emphasis on how it "is," on the subjective appreciation of the sensations, an appreciation of the very process of learning.

Male friends or instructors may be exasperated when we "dawdle" on the mountain, but unless they try, they cannot know how it is to slow down and hear the squeak of snow.

"Americans have come to think of achievement in terms of success, in relation to others. Consequently, achievement now connotes achieving more than others can, or winning," say Thomas Tutko and Patsy Neal. "However, if an individual can channel her energies in order to accomplish improved play, for *that* individual it is an achievement and it should be recognized as such."

Such an attitude opens the pleasure and the rewards of skiing to everyone, not simply to those gifted individuals who have good reflexes or strong thighs. Instead of excluding the average woman or man, it lets us all ride the lift of our choice without pressure to follow the unrewarding trail of the Perfect Skier, with no need to feel guilty or inept because we do not ski better.

"Getting to the point," Russell Baker once grumbled in the *New York Times Magazine*. "Everyone is always insisting on getting to the point. Sometimes the space between points is more fun . . ."

If the "point" is learning to ski better, maybe the space between points is enjoying the scenery, enjoying being with friends, enjoying feeling our bodies move gracefully, enjoying learning more about ourselves, enjoying feeling in harmony with our surroundings. Maybe being women gives us an edge on romping in the space between points.

3

How We Learn to Ski

We have armchaired some ideas about why many women are self-conscious or insecure when they ski. We have talked about how women can use skiing to rid themselves of stereotypes which interfere with their lives and how women can help make skiing more pleasurable for both sexes.

Now we must get out of the armchair and onto the hill, stop talking and start skiing, so we can explore some of these new ideas. We want to learn to ski or ski better, to try the spread eagle that Marion Post demonstrated for a magazine or try to get off the beginner hill and onto the intermediate hill.

There are a lucky few among us who will fly off a bump and spread their arms and legs exuberantly in a perfect spread eagle the first time; who will move off the beginner hill and onto the steeper intermediate terrain with confidence and control. Most of us have to learn.

The way we learn a complex motor skill like skiing—or

any part of it such as flying off a bump—is try, try again. And the more we know about why our first trial failed, the better we will do on our second trial.

"It appears that learning is a function of the number of practice trials with knowledge of results," says Virginia Lee Bell in *Sensorimotor Learning.*

We all know about the practice part: "Practice makes perfect." "Groove your stroke." "Physical learning takes place through repetition," says Lito Tejada-Flores in *A Ski Teacher's Handbook.*

But what is knowledge of results? Do we have an announcer standing at the bottom of the slope broadcasting to the crowd, "Sally Jean just did a really rotten spread eagle. Let's hear it for Sally Jean's next trial."

Well, that's one way of finding out. Most of us prefer our feedback a little less public and much more specific. We can get our feedback—our knowledge of results—from many sources. We can get it from a ski instructor, from a friend, from a videotape, even from a book or magazine which describes how a movement should look or how it should feel. But the closer the feedback is to the actual performance, the more valuable it is.

When we are learning a motor skill like skiing, one of the most valuable sources of information is our own bodies. That's called kinesthetic feedback.

Say you are learning to ride a bicycle. You balance a little bit, wobble, and then take a tumble. You know what it felt like while you were balancing. When you try again, you attempt to re-create that feeling. You also know how it felt as you began to lose your balance, so the next time you try to avoid that feeling. In the beginning you are very conscious of trying to compensate for the error that caused you to lose your balance—you don't lean to the side so much, for instance.

"While we are learning a new skill like skiing," says Robert Ornstein in *The Psychology of Consciousness*, "all the complex adjustments and motor movements are somewhat painfully in our awareness. As we progress, as skill becomes automatic, the movements no longer enter into consciousness."

At the point at which it has become automatic, we have learned to ride a bicycle or to ski. We may still have to learn how to ride or ski faster, over bumpy terrain and so forth, but we learn those additional skills in the same way.

When you learn to ride a bike, the "knowledge of results" is pretty easy. Either you balance or you fall.

What happens when the results are not so obvious? Virginia Bell reports on dart-throwing tests. Some of the dart throwers were blindfolded so that they couldn't see how close to the target their darts were landing. Their throws became less and less accurate. We are not blindfolded when we ski, but the knowledge of whether or not we are performing a movement "accurately" is much harder to discern than if we are losing our balance on a bike or throwing a dart. Anything that will sharpen our vision, turn up the volume on the feedback, will help us to learn better. Anything that increases our awareness of the sensations involved with what works and what doesn't will increase our accuracy. A ski instructor can help you do that, help you identify the feelings involved with successful movements.

"Yes," she says. "Now you are edging your skis. Do you feel it?"

You become aware, you tune in to the sensations, to the way your body feels when it is edging the skis. The next time you try to edge, you will try to reproduce those sensations.

Static on the Line: What Causes It?

But there are many things that interfere with our awareness of sensation, that block the feedback from our bodies and our efforts to reproduce success.

You cannot concentrate on what you are doing and how

it feels if your mind is cluttered with other thoughts. If you are wondering whether the people on the chair lift are watching you, if you are thinking about impressing that handsome man, if you are worried about the patch of ice coming up, you cannot be singleminded about what you are doing.

"Ya can't t'ink and hit at da same time," Yogi Berra once said.

Concentrating means staying mentally focused on something.

"One experiences the object and *only* the object of concentration," say Thomas Tutko and Umberto Tosi in *Sports Psyching.*

"The main difference between concentrating and simply having your attention on something for the moment is that concentration is deliberate and controlled and does not move from one object to the next," they continue.

"Because your mind pays attention to only one thing at a time, [stray thoughts] push out the things you were trying to concentrate on."

Part of our problem in learning comes either from not concentrating on what we are doing or from concentrating on the wrong things, like the patch of ice, the handsome man.

Part of our problem comes from "trying hard."

"But," you say, "we are supposed to try hard, aren't we?"

Our society on the whole puts a great premium on trying hard. As Laurence Morehouse and Leonard Gross point out in *Maximum Performance,* "Our tradition holds that the battle is won by the man who gives to the limit. We deify sacrifice. Death is the ultimate performance.

" 'He killed himself' is a colloquial form of flattery. . . . In working life we often rate others' performances in terms of the cost to them. If I give you a job to do that I think is pretty difficult, and you return an hour later with the job well done but with no apparent cost to you in terms of emotional drain and physical energy, I tend not to appreciate that effort."

Giving it "every last ounce," however, interferes with our learning in several ways. First of all, it can interfere with our concentration. "Trying hard" often produces tension and anxiety, mental static. Second, tense muscles do not transmit well. Thus, our feedback is not as clear.

Try this exercise. Get a tennis ball or any object which is round and will roll under your foot. Put your foot on it with your leg relaxed, knee flexed easily, and roll the ball under your foot. Concentrate on the way your foot and leg feel, on the messages being sent. You can almost feel the minute adjustments of the foot and leg, as if the ball is part of you. You are comfortable.

Now tense your leg—thigh muscles, calf muscles, foot. Almost immediately you experience a precarious feeling. The ball is no longer part of you, but a foreign, perhaps hostile object. The messages are not getting through clearly and your whole body gets into the act of picking up and transmitting information, of keeping your leg and foot rolling the ball around.

Tension also interferes with the proper functioning of our muscles.

Muscles work in opposition to each other. When one group of muscles contracts to do the work of moving or lifting, the opposing muscles extend. They stabilize the joint and they prevent the flexing muscles from going too far and causing injury.

In order that the flexing muscles may work efficiently, the opposing muscles must be able to extend, to release. Smooth and efficient movement depends on this. When we try too hard, the extending muscles as well as the flexing muscles tense and prevent optimum functioning.

Try this. Hold your arm straight out at shoulder height. Now bring your hand toward your head, bending the elbow. Stay loose; do it a couple of times. Now tense your arm. Tense all of the muscles and try to bring your hand toward your head. The movements are jerky, the arm shakes with the effort. You're trying too hard, "giving every ounce."

Trying hard doesn't work. It kicks off a cycle of frustration and defeat. We want to be good so we try hard, become anxious as we try, do badly because we are tense, and become more anxious.

What does work is learning "to relax and get fully into the action," as Tutko puts it.

Many of the exercises used in Woman's Way classes, as well as in other instruction methods that imply a "humanistic" approach, have to do with helping the student to relax and get fully into the action.

To a great extent, traditional instruction, which asks students to do something "right" and thus opens the possibility of her doing it "wrong," puts pressure on her—makes her "try." If instead, we tune in to our subjective sensations, there can be no "right" or "wrong."

In Chapter 5 (What to Do About It) we describe some exercises that will help you to relax and tune in to what you are actually doing. Often when the exercises are introduced in a Woman's Way class, a student's face lights up with discovery.

"Very interesting," said Carol. "I am feeling all sorts of new things. I never really knew I had feet before."

Errors Are Part of the Action

Another thing that interferes with our awareness, with our learning is our tendency to obliterate our errors. Because we are brought up to think that mistakes are wrong, we want to pretend that mistakes never happened. We don't see what we don't want to see—we block out our mistakes. By blocking out our errors, we lose the opportunity to learn from them. We either repeat them or overcompensate for them.

Mistakes are part of the learning process. We do not learn without mistakes. If we lose our balance on a bicycle and block out why we have lost our balance, we cannot correct our error. If we do not tune into the feeling of being off-balance, then we cannot truly understand how it is different from being balanced. If we lose our balance and cover up our error by berating ourselves or by reciting verbal directions from a technical manual, then we have lost the opportunity to learn from the error.

When a baby learning to walk totters and falls over, she doesn't say to herself, "Okay, clumsy, remember what it said on page three and lean a little more to the left now." She tunes in to the way her body feels.

"I don't like that feeling," her body says, and automatically makes an adjustment. "How's this one?"

Elissa and a friend were sitting on a beach talking and enjoying the day. Elissa idly picked up some rocks and began throwing them at a piece of wood.

"As we talked," Elissa reports, "I continued throwing and my accuracy increased enormously. My friend noticed this, and I told him what I'd been doing.

"On the first throw, I knew it was going to miss the piece of wood, so I looked away as it fell and dismissed it. Then I realized 'practice what you preach.' I wasn't learning by my mistake. So the next time I threw I looked at where the rock landed and estimated to myself the distance I had missed and in what direction. I did not try to adjust for the miss, just noted it carefully and left it up to my body to make the proper adjustment. Soon I was throwing more and more accurately. It was absolutely fascinating to watch my body making the compensations without my directions.

"My friend gave it a try. He threw the rock and called out how far from the piece of wood and in what direction the rock had landed: Six inches to the left, three inches to the right. He was looking closely at his error, defining exactly what it was.

"But with me there he had an additional benefit because

I was helping him correct his estimates. At first, he exaggerated the distance.

"We tend to exaggerate our mistakes. You know, we say 'I missed by a mile' when what we mean is six inches.

"He would say six inches when it was three; three inches when it was one. So I helped him by giving my estimate after his estimate. He began to see the exaggeration and became more accurate in his estimates. After he was hitting the wood fairly consistently, he remarked on how relaxed he had felt throughout.

"That's because for one thing he was engrossed in what we were doing, not in trying to hit the wood. But also the pressure was off him. It was an experiment we were trying, and if the experiment didn't work that showed the experiment wasn't effective, not that he was a bad rock thrower or uncoordinated."

This kind of awareness, awareness of what we are actually doing, is called nonjudgmental awareness. We see our mistakes carefully, but we don't make ourselves anxious by calling them "bad."

Elissa first learned these concepts in a tennis clinic being given by Timothy Gallwey, author of *The Inner Game of Tennis* and co-author of *Inner Skiing*. Its application to learning to ski is evident.

If you come off a bump practicing your spread eagle and you land with a jolt and fall, you can tell yourself, "Boy, am I clumsy," pick yourself up and try again. You will probably land with a jolt and fall again.

But if you were very aware of how your body felt—how rigid your knees were, for example—as you landed, then you are estimating your distance from the wood. Next time you may fall again, but your body will begin to adjust and you'll come closer to how it feels to land without falling. If you have an instructor or a friend who can help by confirming or correcting your own estimates of exactly how much your knees were flexed, then you'll probably learn faster, with fewer trials.

Say your turns are taking you too much uphill for your

taste. You want to stay a little closer to the fall line, to link your turns sooner. Note how much you're turning out of the fall line with each turn: a lot, a little, less, a little more, a lot less, a lot more.

You are sitting back more than you want to. Be aware of yourself and estimate how much you are sitting back; really way back on your heels, a little less, more on the center, and so forth.

Don't make a conscious attempt to change. Try trusting your body to make the adjustment.

Exaggerate your errors. What do you like least about your skiing? You skid your turns? Skid them as much as you can; really exaggerate the skidding.

You feel off-balance. Make yourself more off-balance. As one student laughed, after she tried it, "You can't be more off-balance and still stand up." In the process, she found a balance point.

One bleak day an entire class announced to Elissa that they were all skiing "crummy."

"Okay," said Elissa. "Let's rate our crumminess. Ski crummy, crummier, crummiest."

The "crummy" class was, in fact, simply feeling lethargic and uninterested. In the process of exaggerating "crumminess," the whole exercise became so silly that they relaxed, laughed, and their interest was aroused again.

By exaggerating your error, you see what it is you are doing to cause it. Once again, there need be no conscious effort to correct it.

One of the functions of a ski lesson is to help us put our awareness where it has to be put, either to acquiring a new skill or to our errors, because, very often, we don't know that they are errors. Errors feel "right" to us because we are used to them. They are only wrong because they are less effective than doing it right, but we don't know that yet.

Skiing is such a totally new experience for most of us that we often have no kinesthetic reference. And because we are tense, cold, and frightened in the beginning, we rely on old established responses to new messages which are probably not coming in very clearly because we are tense, cold, and frightened.

Thus, as we begin to slide down the hill, we fear we are going to fall so we swing our shoulders and/or hips around to bring the skis across the hill and stop them. A good many times—six out of ten—this will do the trick; it will stop the skis. Our behavior has been rewarded by success. We will incorporate that behavior into our repertoire of skiing maneuvers. Do it often enough and it will feel "right." Your body gets used to skiing that way.

Dinah discovered, for instance, in a Woman's Way session on "What-am-I-really-doing-when-I-think-I'm-doing-something-else" that she frequently skied with her weight back, way back. It felt good to her; it felt "right." It was a posture that was also responsible for a lot of falls she took on moderate and even easy slopes. She pushed her weight forward and discovered—eureka!—that she felt as stable as a rock. She felt really "right."

In a sense, the person who sticks with a mistake has no choice. Plan A worked. She has had no exposure to Plan B and so doesn't know that it works better. Her "knowledge of results" is only partial. There is no basis of comparison. A ski lesson will at least present the options.

It works for experts as well as beginners. Former racer Holly Brown was teaching a series of discovery exercises in a Woman's Way seminar. She had been using a new pair of skis for a week and had been standing on them in a position which was appropriate for her old skis. The new skis had not been performing as they should and she was ready to give them up in disgust. Doing the exercises with the students, she discovered what she called "a whole new place on her skis" where she felt comfortable and stable, and which made the new skis work for her.

Once you have learned a new skill or have repatterned an old habit, once you have the right feeling, then practice does make perfect. You will want to practice that skill until the memory is in your body, until you've "grooved" the skill deeply enough into your nerve pathways and muscles so that when you get into trouble, you won't fall back into your old habits.

But be patient with yourself. Changing bad habits takes time. Given enough practice, the nerve pathways will be grooved, the muscles will remember, and the skill will become automatic. You will have "learned" it.

As we learn, it helps to keep in mind that motor learning is not linear. We are often victims of our Western patterns of thinking. We are trained to think in logical constructs: A follows B and is the cause of C. That may be true in law or logic but it is certainly not true in motor learning. One good turn does not necessarily lead to another; one bad turn does not necessarily deserve another. There is a progression from one turn to another, but it is not necessarily in a straight line.

Stu Campbell of the Professional Ski Instructors of America suggests that our learning progresses in a spiral, like a corkscrew. Our learning pattern goes up and down and maybe backward before it moves forward.

So don't be discouraged if you take two steps backward, one step forward and turn a somersault before you advance to Boardwalk. It's the way people learn a motor skill.

How to Shortcut Trial and Error

Imitating a good athlete is the best way for many (though not all) people to shortcut some of the trial and error. That is the reason why instructors demonstrate and why we follow them down the hill. It helps to follow any good skier or even to watch a good skier from the chair lift or the top of the slope.

Even when we stand still and watch a demonstration without attempting to imitate the movements, our bodies begin to rehearse it subtly. If you have ever gone to a dance concert or a baseball game and felt your muscles twitch faintly as the ballerina did an arabesque or the pitcher wound up, you may have felt your body "rehearsing" subliminally.

In the beginning, the skier who learns by watching is only capable of absorbing the gross aspects of a new movement. If you are starting to learn carved turns, for instance, and you watch the instructor demonstrate, you may see and imitate only the transfer of weight and the position of the body. Later as you become more skilled, you may absorb the subtler movement of the legs and degree of edging.

Another means of rehearsing without actually practicing on the hill is called visualization. Visualizing is a process used by many competitive athletes. It is like running a movie in your head, a videotape of yourself or someone whom you want to imitate performing a maneuver or a run. Dr. Richard Suinn of Colorado State University has worked extensively with ski racers. He has observed, generally speaking, that those who visualize most effectively win.

Before a race, all ski racers think about the course, planning every turn, picking the fastest line. Those who do it best literally ski the course in their minds. It takes as long to run the course mentally as it does in reality. They see themselves so clearly that they may catch an edge coming through a gate. Then they rerun the film, come through the gate again, correcting the error.

Jack Nicklaus in *Golf My Way* describes how he visualizes his golf shots in reverse: He sees (in his mind's eye) where the ball has landed, then the ball flying through the air to where it will land, then himself making the shot which will send the ball on its way.

"It's like a color movie," he says.

In the dart-throwing tests described by Virginia Bell, a number of students were divided into three groups. All three groups were tested and then sent home. The first group was told not to practice at all; the second group to practice physically throwing thirty-five darts a day and the third group to practice mentally for fifteen minutes a day. All three groups returned in twenty days to be tested again. The group that did not practice showed no significant improvement. But groups two and three each showed about the same amount of improvement. Other tests with other skills verified the result.

The conclusion was that mental practice was as effective, or nearly as effective, as physical practice.

Elissa wondered for years why she skied better the first day of the season than she skied for weeks afterward. Then she realized that all summer whenever she pictured herself skiing, she was always skiing beautifully. She never pictured mistakes, hesitations or falls. This was the body language she carried with her to the first days of skiing in the winter.

When we visualize, the closer we can get to the actual experience, the better. Use the same amount of time to visualize a turn as you would take to make it on the hill. Reproduce the sensations of the movement as well as the positions of the body.

Visualize yourself in your best, most satisfying run. Do it slowly, as you would actually do it on the hill. While taking a lesson, watch your instructor with soft eyes, as if you were watching a movie. Don't pick apart her movements. Try and let the movements groove in your body. Then visualize them, perhaps as you ride the chair. Mental practice helps make perfect.

Tune in to your errors as you visualize. As you run the movie, if you sense something is wrong, stop the picture and look at yourself. Ah, you see that you are not shifting your weight to the outside ski early enough in the turn. Make the proper weight shift mentally. Edit your film. It will translate to body language.

Understanding Body Language ━━━━━━

Body language is different from regular language.

There are two basic ways we learn and function. One way is verbal, analytical, sequential. We read this sentence from left to right, one word after the other, and understand its meaning. This is our intellectual side.

The other way is nonverbal, feeling, holistic; we apprehend things all at once in their entirety. Look around your room. You are seeing the entire room. You are not seeing the sofa + the rug + the lamp + walls = the room.

This is our intuitive and creative side.

The brain is divided into two hemispheres connected by a tissue called the corpus callosum.

It has been found through work with brain-damaged people in whom the connecting tissue has been severed by accident that the two hemispheres of the brain to a great extent divide these functions, these ways of learning and apprehending the universe, between them. The left hemisphere of the brain controls the right side of the body. It also controls the verbal, intellectual, analytical functions in most of us. The right hemisphere controls the nonverbal, intuitive, spatial functions.

When we are talking about body language, we are talking about a skill dominated by the right hemisphere.

We learn using both modes, both sides. It would seem silly to teach a child to add by asking her to "feel" the sums of two plus two. On the other hand, it would be just as silly to teach her to walk by explaining analytically and in sequence how to walk. We are best able to express our potential when we let each mode handle its appropriate area and learn from each.

For example, you are watching an instructor demonstrate a turn. Rather than just "seeing" it you give yourself directions as it goes along: "Now she is lifting her arm, now she is moving it forward, now she is moving her wrist so that the pole is aimed forward." She would be over the hill and gone before you could verbalize the series of movements.

"In skiing, an attempt to verbally encode each bodily movement would lead to disaster," says Robert Ornstein.

Try driving a car that way. "Press foot on accelerator, listen to the engine rev, now shift into gear, steer a little to the right, now a little to the left, now take foot off the accelerator and get ready to make a turn." By the time you mentally verbalize those directions and perform them in sequence, you will have crashed out of the driveway into your neighbor's house.

Instead, the way we drive is to decide (left brain) where we want to go. Then we start the car and we automatically make the motions (right brain) which will get us there. The right brain, the intuitive self, takes over the body movements; the left brain, the analytical self, makes the judgments.

We operate most efficiently when we use both sides of the brain, each assigned its appropriate task. In our society, however, it is the left-brain function, the intellectual, that is revered. The right brain, the intuitive, is not.

In the rock-throwing incident above, it was the left side that estimated the distance the rock was landing from the target, the right side that was responsible for the adjustments we made. For most people, it would take a conscious effort to keep the analytical part of us from interfering. "More to the right," it would say. We do not have enough trust that our intuitive part will make the connection.

As Denise McCluggage says in *The Centered Skier*, "Being reasonable and logical are desirable attributes; being intuitive is a little spacey. There is foot-shifting in its presence. It is not asked to address the graduating class and no doctorates are granted in its name. . . . In our wordy world, the very muteness of the right hemisphere has perhaps kept it from proper appreciation."

Interestingly, it is the left-hemisphere activities— analysis, logic, words—that are considered more "masculine," the right-hemisphere activities—intuition, emotion, gesture—more feminine.

The fact that the left brain is so highly valued in our society and the right brain so underrated is another indication of how masculine values dominate. To strike a balance, to create a healthy whole, we should value more highly the right hemisphere.

In skiing this means trusting our intuitive side, our body language, to integrate the skills and respond to messages without constant direction and control. The ski instructor who teaches by keeping the class on the side of the hill while she carefully explains the technicalities of the maneuver she is about to teach is giving in to the verbal-analytical side of herself. She would do better to demonstrate the maneuver and use her words to suggest images the body can imitate.

The way we learn best from verbal directions is to translate them into a mental image. For example, the instructor or a book describes the way to edge your ski in a turn: "As you step onto the new outside ski, feel a light pressure under your arch; as the turn progresses, push the arch into the snow even harder, at the same time pushing the inside of your ankle toward the snow."

What to do, if you are tuned in to the right brain, is form a picture in your mind of what those words mean. It may be a metaphoric picture, a vision of yourself doing a dance step on the slope, a Fred Astaire-Ginger Rogers routine which calls for a lot of ankle action. Or it simply may be a picture of you doing what the instructor has just described.

It is the image that you learn from.

There are times in learning when those analytical words are necessary. It is helpful, for instance, to many of us to understand with our intellectual side why we are learning this particular skill and what we are expected to do. Some of us feel more secure having the purpose and the mechanics of a skill explained before we abandon the left brain.

We do need our whole brain to function in learning to ski, to drive a car, to swim. It is not valuable, as the authors of *Skiing from the Head Down* point out, "to send your brains out for a beer" when you take to the ski slope. The head and body work best in harmony.

But too much verbal direction is a trap. Verbal directions interfere with our awareness of what is actually going on, with what we are feeling and sensing; they clutter the mind.

Convert words to images and, as McCluggage says, "Forebear converting image to words."

Watch skiers and other instructors holistically without breaking apart what they are doing. That doesn't mean you always have to watch the whole body. If you are interested in what the knee is doing or in how the turn starts, then focus on the knee or the start of the turn. But watch it with your whole body and let your body absorb the motion.

Empty your mind. Make more room for body language.

Part of the reward of learning to ski is finding out about ourselves. How do we learn most comfortably? Some of us are watchers, some tryers, some need a sprinkling of analysis. We can enjoy the sense of self-discovery that comes with realizing that the process of learning, of trying and trying again, is more than half the fun. In finding out that we can learn body language fluently, or that we are bilingual—verbal and intuitive—we have discovered something about ourselves that will help in other parts of our lives. If we focus only on the next goal and not on the learning itself or the process of discovery, we negate much of the joy of the experience and miss a good deal of information about ourselves and our skills along the way.

Suppose Christopher Columbus had focused only on his goal of discovering a new route to India. He would have come upon the new continent, realized it wasn't India, and sailed home to report failure. Fortunately, Columbus and others around him realized there was much more to gain from his "failure" than from success.

4

How We Sabotage
Our Own Best Efforts

Many of us spend our lives trying to find out who we are. Some die trying, but happy in the search. Others settle early on for a definition strictly limited to the roles we play: "I am a mother, I am a writer, I am a banker." Few of us begin autobiographies for our class alumnae magazine by announcing "I am a skier."

You would never know this by the way we approach learning to ski. Watch a group of skiers in class or a skier who has just taken a fall or an involuntary 360° spin. They shake their heads and talk to themselves, sometimes pounding their poles, sometimes even crying. They berate themselves for their stupidity, their clumsiness, their failure in performance. The whole world is watching, they have failed, and they might as well go home, sit in a hot tub, and open their veins.

Now, that is absurd.

It is extremely unlikely that you the watcher have even judged the performance, let alone the person who fell. But wait until you get out there and take a fall, make a bad turn, or pull back from a steep slope. Listen to what you tell yourself, to how you punish yourself: "I'm clumsy, I'm a loser, I'll never learn to ski."

We don't stop there. We seize upon our skiing error like Sherlock Holmes seizes upon a piece of lint and submit it as damning evidence that we are guilty in the Whodunnit of life. If we ski badly, we are "bad" people; if we fall, we are "fallen" women.

Elissa believes very strongly—and it is the first lesson in her instructors' training clinics—that the single biggest problem, the root of many of the more obvious obstacles to learning, performing, and enjoying skiing, is the identification of performance with ourselves, with who we are.

Both women and men tend to equate self with skiing performance, but women have their own reasons. Women often have less experience in learning sports skills; they do not realize that it often takes a long time and many errors to acquire a complicated skill like skiing. Even knowing this, many women invest heavily in skiing as a yardstick of their worth: this turn will be the measure of me as a person. When we make a mistake, it is our "fault," our "failure."

Women may turn to skiing because other rewards, the public appreciation of their other activities, are often poor by contrast with those of men. They do not make as much money in their jobs, they do not get promoted as quickly to jobs of responsibility, they are "only" housewives. So they think, "If I can't do anything else, at least I can learn to ski well."

When they can't learn to ski well right away—Zap! That proves what they knew all along: They are failures as human beings.

One of the reasons so many people, women and men, fall victim to this kind of performance pressure is that to some extent our actions do reflect who we are. There are plenty of clichés that testify to that: actions speak louder than words, clothes make the man. Thus, if a woman speaks warmly of her fondness for flowers, but her garden is full of weeds, we know by her actions that she probably likes her flowers via Florist Telegraph Delivery.

A woman tells you she's a so-so skier and then proceeds to carve a flowing track down the area's steepest slope. Her actions belie her words. But we cannot assume that she was being Heephishly humble when she described herself as so-so; maybe her standards of so-so and yours are that far apart. Actions do not tell all.

When we fall, it is not true that our fall proves us to be worthless. The ability to learn to ski is just one of dozens of characteristics which make each of us special. I may be interested in clothes, I may dislike animals, I may have a large appetite, I may be able to multiply four-digit numbers in my head; I may not be able to walk and chew gum at the same time or I may learn motor skills quickly.

Learning to ski is not the sum of who we are. We know that; we've probably even passed that advice along to friends: "It doesn't matter. No one noticed. What will it all matter in a thousand years?"

But it's easier to say that than to tear up the indictments we have prepared. We are very tricky, we skiers. We have an army of saboteurs in our heads, each armed with a device more devious than the one before to undermine our confidence.

Here are some of the things we do to ourselves when we go out to ski:

• We generalize our errors. We put labels on aspects of our performance and transfer those labels to ourselves, just as if we were arranging files or storing jelly jars. "I am not learning as quickly as the rest of the class. I am dumb."

"I can't seem to bring both skis around at the same time. I am uncoordinated."

"The whole class is at the bottom of the hill already. I can't keep up with them. I'm a loser."

• We rehearse catastrophe. We stand at the top of a steep, bumpy run and say to ourselves, "I'm going to fall. I'll never be able to get down this. I'm going to get hurt." Practice makes perfect. Having rehearsed disaster so well in our heads, we do fall and perhaps get hurt.

• We talk ourselves into inertia. There is a stream of advice, admonition, and castigation going on in our heads that makes TV talk show babble sound Socratic. The mind can focus fully on only one thing at a time. We can either ski or give ourselves advice, not both.

Rita was taking a lesson from Elissa and started down the slope after her, skiing smoothly and fast. Midway, she stiffened and slowed down. Elissa asked why. Well, Rita said, she had to slow down to think about what she was doing.

"Think less and ski more," advised Elissa.

It's good advice in any of the above situations.

• We are perfectionists. We don't want just to ski; we want to ski perfectly. We set our standards impossibly high. Not only must we be able to ski those bumps, every turn must be in perfect form. Our friend Barbara, a self-admitted perfectionist, makes a revealing statement. She skis with a group of men, and with the thought always in her mind, "Will they accept me if I make a bad turn?"

• We become overly competitive. We play the game of making the instructor like us more than the other students. Or we must learn faster, better, or ski more smoothly than the woman next to us who is older, younger, dumber, better-looking. Or better than our male companions. The war between the sexes finds a new battlefield. But skiing is not a war game—there's room for us all.

• We exaggerate our fear of making fools of ourselves. Women, who are more sensitive than men anyway to how others perceive them, become hypersensitive on skis. Foolish posture, as in falling or getting up from a fall, is in view of the world. In a book called *Skiing from the Head Down* there is a list of reasons to help psych yourself out of falling: "Falling is cold, uncomfortable, may hurt you, it is difficult to get up, your mother told you not to do anything undignified." All but the last, the authors say, are valid reasons for not falling. The authors are not women.

Our mothers' admonitions to be "ladylike" are still very powerful in women's heads. Face down, behind up in the snow, is definitely not ladylike.

If we can't appear foolish or undignified, then we can never experiment, never challenge ourselves to try something new. If we go out on a limb with a new maneuver, such as a parallel turn, and fail or fall, what are people going to think of us? Better to stick with the perfect snowplow.

• On the other hand, what might happen is that we might succeed in making a fast, clean run down the fall line.

We will have succeeded and succeeded admirably. And many women fear success as much as they fear failure, as Matina Horner's famous study suggested. If we succeed we risk not only emerging from the crowd, losing our safe status as followers, but we risk losing the rewards of failure—comfort and pity, the rewards of a dependent child.

Oh yes, we want to be loved and praised and taken care of. We want to remain children. We spend all our lives trying to grow up, but the temptation to be cuddled is hard to resist. It is as difficult to let go of our own childishness as it is to let go of our children. Sometimes we panic at those moments when we must take responsibility for our own actions, such as the first time we ride a lift alone, the first time we ski without an instructor, our protective authority figure.

Said Erich Fromm: "Man is always torn between the wish to regress to the womb and the wish to be fully born. Every act of birth requires the power to let go of something, to let go of the breast, to let go of the lap, to let go of the hand, to let go eventually of all certainties and to rely upon one thing; one's own power to be aware and to respond. . . ."

• We become "approval junkies." Women tend to view themselves through other people's eyes. We seek approval or at least passive acceptance of our behavior from those around us: Men, other women, bosses, children, even the checker at the supermarket who bestows an approving smile on us because we had the exact change.

This tendency in women is being catered to by a trend in ski teaching that evolves from behaviorism. Behaviorists discovered that positive reinforcements—approval— works better than criticism. Many ski instructors have learned that words of praise make happier students and faster learners. This has in some cases been carried to such extremes that teachers will search for almost anything to praise even if it means saying, "You really fell gracefully that time."

In turn, the student gets so hooked on approval that the

absence of praise becomes a criticism, or they get cynical and discount the approving remarks of the instructor totally.

We need to be able to pat ourselves on the back. We need to feel our own judgment of ourselves is at least as valuable as the grocery clerk's or the ski instructor's.

• We typecast ourselves. We always play the same role no matter what the situation. If a woman has an image of herself as a Magnolia Blossom, she brings that image with her to the ski slope. If she sees herself as an intellectual sharpshooter, she brings her penchant for analysis to the top of the hill.

There is security in the predictability of our own behavior just as there is in that of others. If we know that Anne is always late, then we are not upset when she is late again, although we may be annoyed or inconvenienced. If we know that Ruth is always irritable in the morning, then we are not disturbed if she is irritable this morning. The consistency of the behavior, even if it is unpleasant, is reassuring.

It is reassuring when we act in a predictable way too. If we always get nervous about catching planes, then the feeling of anxiety we get as departure time nears is comfortable in a peculiar fashion because it's the way we always act.

Predictability has value; it enables us to function fairly smoothly in our relationships with others and with ourselves. But if we never exercise other options, we will never know what we can be.

Skiing offers an opportunity to flirt with the charm of unpredictability, to exercise the you that is not Magnolia Blossom. But sometimes we blow it. When we come to the strange world of the ski area, many of us become uncomfortable and insecure. We look for cues on how to behave and take them from the ski instructor or our companions or, if all else fails, from the person we have always been. If we have always been "ladylike," then we behave in ladylike fashion and miss the chance to play with the part of ourselves that is vigorous, assertive, competitive.

• We dwell on our failures. As we think about our last lesson, we see the tumble we took at the top more clearly than the delightful series of linked turns we put together at the bottom. There is a psychological basis for this. In any series of events which is a new and unfamiliar experience, the length of time it takes to integrate it into our consciousness relates directly to the success we have had.

For instance, we are trying a new recipe for a carrot cake. We follow the recipe precisely, the cake comes out beautifully—it is a success. We think no more about the process of making it, except to accept the compliments or enjoy the eating of it. It is integrated into our mental catalog as a feat which can be accomplished when necessary.

If the cake is a disaster—leaden and tasteless—then we will endlessly review in our minds what we did, what went wrong, until we come to a conclusion. The conclusion could be that it was a lousy recipe to begin with. But if we follow the pattern that many of us fall into with our skiing, the conclusion will be that we are lousy cooks. Because we have spent so much time reviewing the failure, it becomes disproportionately important in our minds and we generalize and transfer the failure to ourselves.

Skiing, especially in the beginning, is one failure after another, just as learning to walk was one fall after another. But learning is, by definition, attempting something we can't do. We don't attempt to learn what we already know. So "failure" needs to be put in perspective.

• We bore ourselves. Because many of us are fuzzy about our capabilities or because we are told that this beginner slope is our limit and we are afraid to do more, we ski it again and again, wondering why we are not enjoying ourselves, wondering why everyone talks about the exhilaration of skiing. What's so much fun about this?

We forget that part of the fun of skiing is risk and challenge. We each have our own limits of challenge, our own challenge thresholds. What is frightening for one person will cause another person to yawn and daydream.

• We scare ourselves. We overestimate our abilities—we set our challenge thresholds too high, perhaps because someone else is telling us "You can do it," perhaps because we misinterpret our fear as a failure. So we put ourselves on a slope too steep or take on a maneuver too difficult for us at this time.

Pick your own limits and remember, challenges are not immutable. If the thrill is gone, you can move to a more difficult slope.

• We try too hard. There is a character, a horse named Boxer, in George Orwell's *Animal Farm*. Boxer deals with all difficulties by saying, "I will work harder." The harder he works, the more chaos and disaster build around him.

Trying harder doesn't work in skiing either as we discussed in Chapter 3 (How We Learn to Ski). It doesn't work psychologically, it doesn't work physiologically.

Muscles contract to perform a movement; in order to perform movement again, they must relax. If you are "overtrying," you are keeping your muscles in a constant state of tension. Communication is blocked and eventually the muscles become fatigued and other muscles—the wrong muscles—take over to help out. Performance suffers—chaos and disaster take over.

For example: You are practicing pole plants. It's not working properly. The pole is being planted too late and too far back, so you are being thrown off balance.

"I'll try harder," you say, "to plant it sooner and farther forward."

You grasp the pole more tightly in your effort, thereby tensing arms and shoulders. Your body is struggling to understand the weird messages it is getting and immediately abandons all efforts to deal with rhythm and timing. As the tense arm moves forward to plant the pole, it brings with it the shoulder and upper body and you are soon swinging your upper body back and forth like a pendulum. Chaos is established; disaster will follow.

As ski technician Stu Campbell says, "Try softer," not harder. Focus on where you want the pole to be and the rest will follow.

• We mistake growing pains for terminal incompetence. When Dinah's daughter was five years old, she used to trip over thin air, literally. She would walk through a room with no impediments in sight, and suddenly stumble and fall. Dinah consulted the neighborhood mother's caucus and her child-rearing library and discovered that all the other five-year-olds were doing it too. According to the experts, they were going through one of their periodic states of disequilibrium.

Children grow in spurts and stages. During the stage when they are growing, changing, taking in new information, developing new skills at a rapid rate, they fall over thin air, physically and emotionally. In the process of mastering the new skills and integrating the new information, they lose control of what they already knew. They have given up the old way but not mastered the new. Blessedly for children and parents, they also go through stages of equilibrium during which new material is successfully absorbed and synthesized and they live with it and enjoy it before moving on to the next stage of growth.

That happens to adults too, perhaps not as rapidly and obviously. It certainly happens on the ski slope, where new information and new skills are presented rapidly. In the process of learning to make a carved parallel turn, we bring with it the security of our old stem christie and achieve a kind of bastard maneuver which has us stumbling over thin air. We are getting in our own way, reluctant to give up the security of the old, lacking faith in our ability to master the new.

Dinah was working on letting her skis carve a turn, but she was throwing her hip around to complete her turns, protecting herself in case the new maneuver didn't work. Suddenly in the middle of a run with Elissa, she stopped with the hip and her turns smoothed out, her body relaxed.

"What happened," asked Elissa later.

"I decided to trust my skis to do what I wanted them to do," Dinah answered.

We can learn to trust our own growth.

We have still other ploys to get in our own way, however.

• We make fun of ourselves, as a Woman's Way student

said, "before anyone else can." We head off the humiliation of being laughed at by laughing first and loudest. But there is a difference between laughing at your foibles and mocking yourself.

To say with amusement "I can never buckle my own boots because I'm afraid of breaking a fingernail" is to laugh at a harmless vanity.

To say "I'm just one of those people who can't buckle their own boots" is another game altogether. This woman has immediately set herself up as an uncoordinated, helpless female who should be forgiven for whatever happens to her on the mountain and can't be blamed for her mistakes. When she does fall, it will reinforce her image as helpless and uncoordinated.

There are wonderfully funny women—we all know at least one—who cover up their own sense of inadequacy and fear by spinning hilarious tales of their gaffes and failures. If they told the same stories about another person—about a friend—they would be faulted for cruelty and heartlessness. We do not mock others; why should we mock ourselves?

• We don't take ourselves seriously as skiers. Here is what we call the Ladies' Day Syndrome. Many ski areas offer "Ladies' Day" programs, usually midweek when the lifts are running empty and the areas want bodies. They offer a bargain package of lifts, lessons, and equipment which are tempting to housewives in the area. These programs are frequently viewed by area managements and ski instructors as a coffee klatsch on skis. Lessons are given and taken, but there is no effort to set up and meet challenges, no exertion, no thrust to improve. The instructor condescends, and the skier permits herself to be condescended to. When at the end of a five-week series of Ladies' Days, no discernible improvement has been made, the "lady" will often say to herself, "Well, it was an afternoon with the girls," and bail out.

If we do not take ourselves seriously as skiers, then no instructor is likely to either. There is nothing demeaning or damaging about an afternoon with the girls, whether it's skiing, playing bridge, or quilting. There is a great deal wrong with pretending that you are learning to ski when you are, in fact, socializing or killing time. Learning to ski takes concentration, persistence, and practice. Dilettantes fall a lot and perpetuate the myth that women skiers are incapable.

• We overdo persistence. This is the Bulldog Syndrome and it can be defined as "I'll learn to ski if it kills me." Some of us hang in there with grim determination, resolved to learn to ski no matter what the cost in pain, inconvenience, and money. Determination is an admirable trait, but it can be joyless and self-defeating. Skiing is recreation, not a survival skill. It's unlikely that you'll need to join James Bond in schussing an Alp to escape the bad guys. If there's no fun in the learning, then there will be no pleasure in the accomplishment.

We may not do all of these things to ourselves at one time. It's difficult, though not impossible, to be afraid of success and afraid of failure at the same time, to give up easily and hang on doggedly simultaneously. But most of us will wince in recognition at many of the self-defeating traps on this list, which is surely incomplete.

At this point we should leave a blank for you to fill in:

> HERE is the clever and insidious way I sabotage my efforts to ski better:

Send it to us, care of Summit Books, and we will add it to the list, and to our ever-growing sense of awe and amazement at the way we human beings manage to get in our own way.

All is not lost, however. The next chapter deals with ways in which to circumvent the sabotage, how to get out of our own way. It's far more painless than you might imagine.

5

What to Do About It

"We have met the enemy and she is us," to paraphrase Pogo, the comic-strip possum.

Now, what do we do about it? How do we go about making friends with ourselves? You can tell yourself "Chin up, shoulders back, I'm okay—we're okay," but that is likely to give you only a stiff neck and shoulders. Admonitions and positive thinking don't work very well when fears, poor self-images, and histories of failure are so firmly attached.

Elissa was riding a lift at a ski area in Vermont with another woman.

"What is it like at the top?" the woman asked casually.

"Icy, cold, and the wind is blowing the snow like a blizzard," Elissa answered.

"Oh, yes," said the woman. "I thought so. I just fall apart in those conditions."

"Oh," said Elissa encouragingly.

"I just took a ski class," the woman continued, "and I

told the instructor how I felt. You know what he said? He told me, 'Don't fall apart.' "

No further discussion was necessary. They both knew that that kind of advice—"Don't fall apart, don't be afraid, don't worry about what other people think"—has about as much impact on a self-conscious skier as the surgeon general's warning on a pack of cigarettes has to an addicted smoker.

Our skiing habits, our images of ourselves as skiers are long held and hard-won. If we see ourselves as falling apart on ice, falling apart is a pattern, a habit that has been established as our behavior for ice. Being positive, telling yourself "I am a wonderful person and I can ski this icy slope," does no good if (1) you do not really believe you are a wonderful person, and (2) you have no experience of success on ice.

Dinah's son has created for himself an enemy of spelling and the English language. When it is time to study twenty words for this week's spelling test or write a book report, he grows tense and hostile.

"How do you spell martyr?" he asks.

"Look it up in the dictionary," she says, thinking to guide him to the tools at hand.

"How can I look it up in the dictionary when I don't know how to spell it," he growls.

How can we look up "confidence" if we don't know whether it begins with a K or a C?

What we want to do first is clear the jungle of psychological underbrush—the rehearsals of disaster, the fears of failure and success, the self-mockery. Then we can talk about ways of reestablishing a warm relationship with your body by relaxing and centering, becoming conscious of the joy of your connection to the mountain and the snow by tuning in to where you are, of vying for an Oscar by role playing the unexplored facets of you, of spelling confidence with a C.

Ultimately, we want to come to a real understanding

that performance is not the person, that what we do on a ski slope has only to do with what we do on a ski slope and not with our jobs, our husbands, our friends, and our public image.

We begin by taking a machete to the psychological debris. The first step toward curing self-consciousness is to become conscious of ourselves. Why are we out here on the snow with these rigid boots and long sticks attached to our feet? Why are we doing this?

If the answer is, "I am doing this because a magazine article said everyone was doing it and my sex life would improve, but I hate every minute of it and I would rather be reading a good book or playing chess at the local chess parlor or taking a dance class," then hang up your skis. You are living a magazine editor's life, not your own. You are taking on someone else's goals, not your own.

Being introduced to skiing by a friend or a magazine article is usually more felicitous. You go along for the ride for a weekend and discover that you do like it, that it's invigorating, fun, challenging to slide down a mountain. You have established your own priority. You have incorporated skiing into your life as one of the activities you want to pursue for your own pleasure.

You are now an addicted skier and want only to ski better, but you don't seem to be making any progress. Think about what it is you want to progress to. What is it that you want out of your skiing experience? Do you want to be able to make a parallel turn? Do you want to be able to keep up with your friends? Do you want to ski like Suzy Chapstick? Do you simply want to ski without fear?

Are those realistic goals? Explore your capabilities honestly. The physical: Do you have any prior experience in sports? Are you strong, in good condition with good reflexes? Or is skiing your only sport, except for an occasional swim or bicycle ride? Suzy (Chapstick) Chaffee works out every day.

The psychological: Do you enjoy competition? The

friends you want to keep up with may race each other to the bottom. Do you want to race? Do you like to "attack" a slope or go with it? Or do you sometimes like one and sometimes the other?

Be realistic with yourself. Accept what is really there.

Many of us set goals on the strength of what we "should" be doing, what we "should" be accomplishing and not what we can or want to accomplish. We want to ski like our instructor or like the skier in the movie we saw at the base lodge. But those skiers ski every day. Forget about them. Exaggerating our own capabilities means we are only doing ourselves a disservice. When we fail to ski like someone in a movie, we will only begin to flagellate ourselves, to call up our images of failure.

We don't need to compare ourselves with anyone else or set any abstract level of performance. Our learning is a very personal process. Recognize your challenge, your potential.

What Woman's Way tries to teach is respect for your own efforts, to take seriously the goals which you set for yourself, and to appreciate your own accomplishments for what they are—real accomplishments. Most of us rarely take the opportunity to look back up at the hill and say, "Wow, I just skied all the way down that hill." We look instead at the next slope in front of us and say, "I can't ski that."

Once you have set your own priorities, then put them away on the top shelf out of sight.

Enjoy Skiing Now

The best way to break into the head games we play with ourselves is to take the spotlight off our goals and simply enjoy the process of doing and learning. The original reason that most of us got into skiing was because it made us feel good, it involved us totally in body and senses. It put us in touch with air, wind, and water, with the parts of nature that for most of us are now only filtered through faucets and air conditioners.

Then we got caught up in improving our performance and lost sight of that aspect of skiing, of the enchantment of our own bodies and what they can do and of the pleasure of acting on or interacting with our environment. We trapped ourselves into seeking approval for our progress.

We need to get back in touch with our bodies, our environment, and in the process let go of "self-improvement." We need to recognize and enjoy the sensation that comes from making a good turn, not wait for a "well-done" from instructor or companion.

"There is more joy in feeling one's edges for the first time," says Elissa, "than in making a turn the instructor says is good."

To do that, to savor sensation, we need to relax. We need to concentrate. We need to expand our awareness both of what we are doing and of what we can do.

The exercises that follow are intended to help women—or men—relax, concentrate, expand awareness, and are all designed to be done on skis, some while standing still at the start of a run, some while moving. Some of them can be rehearsed at home if you choose. These exercises, incidentally, come from various sources, but many of them were collected and modified for skiing by Lyn Ballard, a psychotherapist who loves to ski and who works for Woman's Way as a consultant on stretching mind and body.

Centering

One of the Woman's Way students suggested we should call this chapter "In search of a belly button." That's because many of the relaxation and concentration exercises that Woman's Way uses call for "centering" your body.

There are several ways to regard the concept of centering or finding our centers. One is in the metaphysical sense, the sense in which mystics or students of Eastern philosophies use it, as the place in ourselves where energies accumulate and emanate, as our source of connection with the universe. There is also the physical center, the center of gravity, the center of the body where the large muscles come together.

You can also regard the center as the center of consciousness, the center of the cosmos, or at least the center of the space you are occupying at the moment, be it a room or a mountain. You can think of it purely as a metaphor, as a point on your body which we choose to call the center from which it is more efficient and easier to control movement, to achieve balance, to process messages from your environment. McCluggage says in *The Centered Skier*, "It does not really matter how you think of it, your . . . awareness of it is all that is needed. . . ."

As it happens, whether you are talking metaphysically or physically, for most people it is about the same place, usually slightly below the belly button. When Woman's Way talks about centering, we are for the most part referring to physical centering, finding a posture of balance and stability. The other kinds of centering may follow on their own if all goes well.

Centering is not a static process. Even standing still, we are always centering ourselves, making minor adjustments in balance and posture, moving back and forth, side to side, up and down. Certainly when we are skiing, the center is never still—we are always in search of our belly buttons.

• One of the favorite Woman's Way exercises for becoming conscious of your center is to make a noise which can only be described as grunting. Let in a deep breath and push it out making a loud "unhnnnn" sound. Make it with commitment, so that you can be heard; don't whisper it. Do it again. It should be deep and resounding. The point from which the sound is emanating is approximately your center. Do it while you're skiing and make the "unhnnnn" sound as you complete each turn. Make it deeply from your belly, not high from your chest.

There is nothing that captures the attention of an entire mountain of skiers more than a Woman's Way class grunting its way down a slope. But if you can stick to grunting and keep from laughing, you will find your connection with the mountain has suddenly become stronger, firmer. You will feel all at once that the mountain is your friend, holding you up, not trying to trip you up. You are centered.

• Another centering exercise is to ski as if a beam of light were shooting from your navel. You can imagine a flashlight or a laser or a multicolored gel, but keep the light always pointing in the direction you want to go. If you are skiing down, illuminate the bottom of the slope. This takes some practice, but if you concentrate on lighting your path you will feel more stable and may even sense the power and energy beginning to accumulate in your center.

Breathing

The grunting exercise also helps you remember to breathe. Here are other breathing exercises to help you relax. Most of us, either through dance, Yoga, natural childbirth, or exercise classes, have learned that we should breathe into the abdomen, not into the chest. Here's how: Exhale. Push all the breath out of your body. Push it out, out—pull in the abdomen, pull in the ribs. Force the last bit of air out by saying an aspirant syllable. "Help" is a good word. Now let the new air come in, all the way down to your center. Let your abdomen expand. Make the effort when you exhale; let the breath fill your body on its own.

Just breathing will help break a cycle of anxiety, incidentally. If you are standing at the top of an icy slope and you feel panic setting in, simply focusing on your center and breathing rhythmically will help reduce that heart rate.

• Scan your body for tension. Start at your toes and feel whether the muscles in your toes are tense or relaxed. (You can start at your head, too, or your hands or your center, but it's usually easier to start at one end or the other so you don't miss a spot.) Are your toes curled, digging into the mountain, hanging on for dear life? Uncurl them. Feel ankles, calves, knees—are your knees locked? Feel thighs, hip joints, pelvis, buttocks. Now go to the spine, abdomen, ribs, shoulders—ah, that's where it is for most of us, shoulders like Atlas, burdened with the world. Arms, hands—are you clutching your poles to keep from falling off the mountain? Neck, head, face.

Don't try to relax if you discover tension. Now you are only looking for information—which are the spots in your body that carry the most tension?

Now let your breath in—follow your breath. Be aware of it and follow it with your mind's eye to wherever it's going. Don't try to direct it. Exhale. Let in another breath, but this time direct it to the areas of tension. Are your toes curled? Send your breath down to your toes—don't force it down, just send it along. Now exhale, letting your breath wrap around the tension and bring it up from your toes out into the cold air. Send your breath into your shoulders; exhale and let the tension pour out with your breath. Be cynical if you wish, say it's physiologically impossible. Breath goes into the lungs, not the toes. Do it anyway. It works.

Relaxing

Some of us are so tense when we ski—or when we live—that we don't know the difference between undue tension and normal muscular support. We don't know what being relaxed feels like.

• Try this exercise. Bring your arms and poles up in front of you so you can see them. Now squeeze the pole handles hard, as if you were wringing out a sponge. Relax as if you were letting the sponge fill up with water (don't drop the sponges). Squeeze again. Relax.

Do the same with other parts of your body when you think you might be tense. Tense your shoulders, hard, as hard as you can, with all your might. Hold it, hold the tension. Hold it until you can't hold it anymore, until your shoulders shout, "Let go!" Let go. Drop the world. That's what being relaxed feels like. You can do this exercise while skiing.

• At the start of a run, bend over and let yourself hang, your head and neck completely loose. Shake your head to be sure it's loose and really hanging. Be a laundry bag. Shift your weight back and forth from ski to ski. Let your body move. This loosens your lower back too.

• Stand and center yourself loosely. Now let your breath in as if it were all going into your chest, pushing your chest out, out, like a balloon filling up. Exhale. Now let your breath into your back, pushing out your back. Exhale. Now breathe into your sides, pushing out your ribs. Exhale. Inflate your whole chest, like an inner tube. Think of your chest and back, your upper body, as one of those life-size balloons, where you must blow up the head, then the body, then the legs, until finally the whole thing is filled with air. This exercise really lets your lungs open up.

• Stand still and hug a tree. A big tree. Put your arms out in front of you as if you were giving a big hug to a big tree. Hug it warmly. This stretches the muscles across your upper back. Now clasp your hands behind your back. Keep your arms straight and lift up your clasped hands. You'll feel the stretch in your arms and chest muscles; your lungs will expand too.

• Have a friend lift your shoulders from behind and let them drop toward the snow; lift and drop. Keep at it until they really drop of their own weight and you are no longer lowering them.

• Ski like a rag doll. Pretend you are Raggedy Ann or

Holly Hobby or Snoopy or whatever your favorite rag doll was as a child. Ski a run that way, arms loose, head lolling. Shake yourself like a rag doll being tossed in the air.

• Ski to music. Hum a tune or sing out loud. This is everyone's favorite. Waltzes are popular ("The Blue Danube," "The Skater's Waltz") because the beat is definite; polkas have the same rhythm only faster. "Zip-a-de-doo-dah" and "The Man on the Flying Trapeze" are bouncy. One woman with an overdeveloped sense of irony took off down a steep slope to the tune of "Stayin' Alive." Music not only helps skiers relax—who could be tense doing a Vienna waltz—but helps establish rhythm and timing.

Singing or humming helps keep you breathing too. We all have to tendency to stop breathing when we ski—the tougher the run, the more we hold our breath on turns. As one of McCluggage's students said, "I can't breathe and ski at the same time." Try the grunting exercise, making a loud grunt at the end of each turn, for a few turns. Then change to breathing out on every turn. Racers do it; efficient laborers do it; physiologists say you should exhale not inhale with effort. Don't worry about breathing in; the breath will enter your body. This not only lets you breathe and ski at the same time, it helps establish a rhythm.

Concentration, Focusing, Awareness

Having practiced one or some or all of the relaxation and breathing exercises, you are now so loose that you could flow down the hill like molasses. Fine, go ahead and do it. Forget what comes after. You don't need it.

If, however, your body is loose but your head is still playing games with you, if you are, for instance, afraid of success, afraid you're going to ski this run too well or cannot get the memory of the last time you crashed out of your mind, here are some exercises to clear your head.

Self-consciousness, competitiveness, need for approval, all those saboteurs we talked about before, get in the way of skiing even if our bodies are relaxed. If you are worried about what other skiers are thinking of you, you are not thinking about your skiing, you are thinking about other skiers. If you are thinking about how bad (or even how good) that last turn was, you are not thinking about this turn, now. If you are giving yourself directions, "Bend the knees, weight forward, plant pole," you are not thinking about what you are doing, but what you should be doing. You are skiing someone else's run, not your own; making someone else's turn, not your own.

Most of the exercises we talk about next have two purposes: They were developed or introduced into the Woman's Way classes to polish specific skills and to focus attention on the "now." They help the student tune into what she is really feeling and doing and take her mind off what she feels she "should" be doing.

Because some of the exercises are either so silly (as in "grunting") or so simple, there is no possible way they could be "right" or "wrong." Most students forget to ask their instructors for a pat on the head, find it impossible to worry about what other people think. What could they think except "What kind of new game is that?" Elissa even uses these exercises to train instructors because it relaxes them. They let go of the feeling that someone is evaluating them as a good skier-bad skier, or thinking, "Oh, she's a ski instructor and she made a bad turn." They're doing something besides trying to ski well—practicing this weight exercise—so they can be excused for whatever goofs they make (in case you think ski instructors don't feel performance pressure and need approval).

Incidentally, do these exercises, at least in the beginning, on a slope where you are comfortable and confident. You are exploring, practicing, tuning in—this is not the time to challenge yourself. That comes later.

• Ski super slow. Ski as if you were under water, as if you were the star of a slow-motion sequence. Now tune in to what your body is doing. Don't make judgments, right or wrong. Just tune in. Turn up the volume on your arms. Are they forward or back. Where is your upper body, forward or back? Moving back and forth, side to side, absolutely still? Your center: Is it moving or still? If it's moving, how and how much. Knees? Ankles? Toes? Are you breathing? In slow motion? Make some changes but still in slow motion. Drop your arms back. What happens? Bring them forward. What happens?

Exaggerate your shoulder movement. How does it feel? Keep your shoulders still. How does it feel?

Bend your knees more. Straighten them a little. Straighten them a lot. Slow motion, remember. How does that feel? Try to be specific. Don't just say, "It feels funny." What does feeling funny mean? Unstable? Out of control? In control? Awkward? Different? Tune in to only one part of the anatomy at a time. Don't try to think about arms *and* knees or even arms and hands.

• Rock around the sock or exploring leverage. Stand still for this first. Now rock back and forth, first forward slowly, then to the middle, then back. Focus on your foot. Feel your foot as you move back and forth. Identify where the pressure is on your foot as you rock—ball, arch, heel, in between. Now ski, still tuned in to your foot. Where is the pressure? Always in the same place? Moving back and forth? Mostly in the same place?

Where do you feel it most? Increase the pressure there. What happens? Now move forward or back. Increase the pressure. What happens? Keep exploring. Where do you feel most comfortable most of the time? Ski instructors are always telling you to keep your weight forward. Rocking helps you know what that feels like and lets you decide for yourself where you are most stable and well balanced. It's not the same for everyone.

This kind of exercise also helps a skier tune in to the amount of pressure needed to edge the skis: explore increasing pressure on the pad behind the big toe, the inside of the arch, the heel.

• Ski by number. "Bend zee knees, two dollars please" is the way skiers summed up the ski instruction of yesteryear. You can tell how yester the year was by the price of the lesson. But fifteen dollars and twenty years later ski instructors are still telling us to bend our knees and ankles. The problem a lot of women have is that they think they *are* bending their knees and ankles and they think they're bending them a lot. They are not getting or cannot evaluate the feedback. One way to check what is actually happening to your knees or your ankles as you bend is to put a value on the bend. Set your range from 0 to 5, for instance. Standing straight up, with no bend at all, is a 0; bending them as far as they can possibly go is a 5. Now ski a little, calling out where your knees are within that range: 1, 2, 3. Experiment. Push them into a 5. Stiffen into a 0. Try a 1, 2, 3, 4. Where is it most comfortable? Do you always ski a 2 or 3? Is it sometimes more comfortable at one place than another? It should be. If you always ski with your knees or ankles in the same position, you are not responding to the variations in terrain or in your posture.

Try the same number game with edging the skis. Stand in a traverse, skis across the hill. Put a value from 1 to 5 on the amount your skis are edged. Number 1 would be having the skis so flat that you sideslip down the hill; 5 would be edging your skis into the hill, digging the edges in as hard as you possibly can. Now ski across the hill, calling out loud the amount of edging you're doing; experiment edging from 1 to 5. Make another couple of traverses to be sure you have the hang of it.

Now take a run down, calling out the value as you ski. Don't try always to ski a 5 or always ski a 3 or to ski anything in particular; just identify where your edges are as you ski. (It helps to do this with a friend or instructor. She can verify that you aren't just mumbling numbers as your mind drifts off, but that you are actually doing what you say you are doing.)

• "Where is your weight?" is a variation of the number game. Ski across the hill, tuning in to which ski your weight is on. Left or right? Call it out: "Left, left, right, right, oops."

Go back to that oops: What happened? Don't just say to

yourself, "I made a mistake." Was it a mistake? Did another skier cut too close? Was there a bump or a rut you hadn't noticed? Did you call out left when you meant right? What was the oops all about? How did your body feel?

All of these exercises help you discover what you are really doing when you ski, as opposed to what you think you are doing or what you "should" do. They also lead to experiments with what you can do. When you move back and forth in the rocking exercise, for instance, you are letting your body know its options. If you habitually ski with your weight back, as many do, it may be that your body didn't know any other way to ski. This was the appropriate posture for skiing. Now you have informed your body that there may be other postures that are acceptable for skiing. You are free to choose.

You have made yourself aware of what you are doing and of what you can do. Awareness is the key to efficient learning and efficient performance. You are tuned into what you are doing, not how you are doing it. You are now processing the right kind of information to make changes in your skiing. Now when you say, "I am bending my knees," you know they are bent and how much. That much may not be enough, but at least you know where you are.

Tune in to Where You Are

Another way to take our minds off our performance—off the thousands of eyes we imagine watching from the chair lift—is to pay attention to our environment. This does not mean stopping every third turn to admire the view or appreciate the snow crystals on the trees, although that is certainly part of the pleasure of skiing. It means tuning in to the piece of terrain that you are occupying now, even as you ski. It means nurturing a healthy give-and-take with the mountain you are touching and which is touching you, instead of fertilizing a fantasy with the ghost riders in the chair.

• Listen to the sound of the snow as you make a run. Most of us know the chatter of skis on ice, but have you ever listened to the slither of skis in powder or soft pack? The nice satisfying crunch of breaking through a slight crust. It can even turn into a kind of sonata, as you move from a patch of ice to ball bearings to good snow, as you carve or skid or run flat out. Besides taking your mind off whether the guy you met on the lift line is really going to call you for a drink, it feeds you useful information about what you are actually doing. A skidding ski makes a sound different from a carving ski, for instance, as skis on ice have a sound different from skis on hard pack. You will begin to make adjustments in your skiing almost unconsciously.

• "Feel" the texture of the snow. Don't judge it as good or bad snow, but simply observe it clinically. The snow is heavy and wet here, but over there in the shadow it is still packed and dry. What happens when you ski one and then the other?

Feel the wind in your face or the sun on your body. If you're skiing bumps, try to fall into the rhythms of the skiers who went before and made the bumps. See if you can get into their bodies and make their turns.

Role Playing

We have talked about how we limit our actions by our self-image. We see ourselves as passive or aggressive, as thoughtful or inconsiderate, as soft or tough. Most of us are all of these things or have the capacity for all of these things, but once we have selected the image that each of us calls "me," we rarely dip into the well of other qualities. There is security in consistency.

But, as Ralph Waldo Emerson said, "A foolish consistency is the hobgoblin of little minds."

Skiing is a wonderful opportunity to chase away that particular hobgoblin, to expand our minds by exercising our otherwise sedentary attributes.

Think of yourself as a repertory theater. The plays you usually produce feature only one or two characters, the roles you play at home and work. Compelling and worthy characters perhaps, but dulled by frequent repetition. Add a new character on stage, and the play takes on new life and new excitement. Its potential for amusement or education or enjoyment has expanded geometrically.

We can expand ourselves and our skiing experience by adding and subtracting characters. We can experiment with role playing on the slopes. The results of this exercise can be spectacular.

Elissa remembers particularly a student who, although she was technically more accomplished than other people in her class, was also cautious, slow, and unself-confident. The class began to role play and Dolores did pick an aggressive role as the class took run after run. Elissa stopped midway down the hill to watch the class; she was partially screened by some trees. Elissa saw Dolores coming down the hill really going for it, making short little turns, planting her pole aggressively. Dolores saw Elissa and stopped.

"I can't do this," she said.

Another self-styled timid skier also chose the aggressive and confident roles.

"I love playing those kinds of skiers. It was so much fun. I could do anything I wanted to, because it wasn't me," she volunteered.

Wrong. She was wrong and Dolores was wrong. Who, after all, was making those turns; who was chewing up the hill. Not sheep in wolf's clothing, but women who could be either wolf or sheep as the occasion demanded.

There are other ways to play the theater game. Ski like someone you want to be: as precise as your ski instructor, as funny as Carol Burnett, as sexy as Raquel Welch, as political as Walter Mondale, or as elegant as Baryshnikov.

Do all of these games and exercises with abandon. When we approach something new, we tend to be cautious. But if we want to role play at being uninhibited, then it does no good being a little uninhibited. It's like life. We cannot move in with a lover only on weekends and know what it's really going to be like living with him. Without commitment, without risk, no real growth is possible.

"Commitment," Elissa shouts to a student, "with commitment."

You won't make a dent in a hunk of cheese if you simply stroke the knife along the top. You won't make a scratch in grooving new nerve pathways or banishing old ghosts if you are role playing at being aggressive and you clench your jaw like Clint Eastwood but let the rest of your body pick its way down the slope like Woody Allen. Be aggressive from your scalp to your toenails. If you don't like that role at the end of the run, then nothing is lost. Pick another role. Or another exercise. Or another lover . . .

Imaging

Related to role playing is an exercise called "imaging." Imaging calls on body language.

We cannot learn a complicated motor skill like skiing by verbalizing the directions as we ski. We need to incorporate the movements and the sequence of movements into body language, just as we incorporated the skills of walking, running, driving a car. Because we are verbally oriented, we may begin to learn a ski manuever by listening to directions. But we must then translate these directions into an image. It is the image we learn from.

If an instructor says, "Transfer your weight at the beginning of the turn to the outside ski," you picture this in your mind. You get an image in your head of starting the turn and transferring the weight. If you were wired up with electrodes, they would indicate that not only do you have an image in your head, but your body is already beginning to rehearse the movements. It is already beginning to translate and encode the information into body language; the muscles involved are stimulating the electrodes.

One of the best ways to bypass the translation from

mouth to muscle is to watch a skier perform the movements you want to do. As you are watching, your body begins to rehearse the movements the model skier is making. It rehearses first the gross movements and later, as they are mastered, begins to pick up the subtler movements. That is why, in teaching beginning skiers, good instructors will exaggerate their movements.

That is also one reason children learn motor skills so quickly. They do not have the vocabulary or the grasp of abstract concepts to analyze and verbalize. They understand with their bodies, they see with their bodies. They do not filter the image through their intellectual side and retranslate it into body language. They do not break each movement into pieces but see it as part of a whole. But we are adults, and we already have the habit of analysis, the compulsion to relate cause and effect. We need to reinstate or reinforce our ability to image.

Pick an image. Start with a simple word, a single quality. Ski like silk. Get an image in your mind of a silken banner rippling down the hill. Feel your body already begin to soften and slide even before your skis move. Now slink silkily down the hill. Repeat the word if you want to.

Be an animal. Ski like a black panther—picture a black panther in your mind. Ski like a puppy. If you're facing a mogul field, ski like a mountain goat. Or like a snake. It is amazing how quickly your body will respond to the image. It doesn't matter whether at the end of the run, your partner recognized that you were a black panther; you know what you were.

Ski behind the best skier you have ever seen. If she's there on the slope with you, good. Then fall in behind her. If not, put the image in your mental projector. Don't analyze what she's doing, just be her. Let your body be her shadow.

You can do this with bad skiers too, simply to get the kinesthetic feeling of being off-balance or overturning.

Visualizing, a form of imaging which calls on memory rather than imagination, is discussed in Chapter 3 (How We Learn to Ski).

The exercises in this chapter are not meant to teach you how to ski. For that you need to be taught new skills, refine others, incorporate movements. What these exercises are meant to do is help relieve the pressure to "perform," fine-tune awareness, develop your body vocabulary and integrate new skills. More important, they help you develop independence as a skier and as a student. You begin to take responsibility for your own learning, not to be dependent on an instructor to tell you what to do and to praise you for doing it right. You learn what "right" feels like for you. Because the feeling is good, there's no longer any need to compare yourself with instructor or classmate or friend. You set your own goals in your own terms.

In the process, you learn to trust yourself and your own feelings, to know what is right for you. You learn to trust your body to incorporate new skills.

Along the line we should also learn to abandon reproach and admonishment, learn to praise ourselves for what we have accomplished. Look up at the icy slope you just skied down. That was terrific; you couldn't do that last week or last winter.

That sense of self-appreciation was personified by a skier in a Woman's Way seminar who began the week—as many did—by considering herself inept, uncoordinated. Skiing had come to be all effort and no pleasure.

At the end of the week, coming down off the mountain on the last run of the day, Dinah fell in behind her and played the game of being her. Her rhythm was smooth and silken, her body, as Dinah captured the feeling in her own, relaxed and almost sensuously connected to the snow. They stopped at the ski racks. "Melody," Dinah said, "that was beautiful."

"I know," she said.

That was her accomplishment. Not the improvement in her skiing, but the ability to experience the pleasure, the moment, and to accept it as her own. She had made friends with herself.

6

Taking a Lesson

With all our newfound skills of relaxation, concentration, and awareness, why bother to take a lesson? We'll just keep skiing and pretty soon we'll be perfect.

Maybe.

Maybe not.

Because even with all our newfound confidence, skiing is still a complex sport that involves complicated skills. It is helpful to shortcut our way to those skills by having someone who already knows how to pass on what she's learned. It is helpful to have someone give us feedback about what we are doing, as opposed to what we think we are doing.

Why should we want to improve? Isn't it enough fun just to be able to ski and enjoy it—to relax and have fun now that we have tuned in to our bodies? It sure is fun. If that is what is giving you pleasure, hanging loose in your turn and not worrying anymore about what other people are thinking, then enjoy it. We mean it when we say choose your own goals and the way you want to ski.

But most people find that one of the benefits of skiing is

being able to grow in the sport. The challenges to be dealt with and overcome enhance the thrill of skiing. We want to be able to ski from the top of the mountain, to ski ice, to ski powder, to do a flip or a ballet maneuver. To move from a wedge turn to a parallel turn, to flow down a slope instead of hacking our way down. A skilled instructor can help us clarify those challenges, direct our awareness to where changes should be made, and teach us new skills for new maneuvers.

Instructors are trained to be good detectives. If you frequently "catch an edge" there may be any number of reasons for it. A good instructor can save a lot of time by helping you focus on where the error is most likely to be.

A good instructor can help us crystallize the next challenge. You want to ski faster? That's pretty vague. Faster than who? Faster than your sister? Faster than you usually ski? Why don't you ski faster? It may be that you are skiing as fast as you can for the skills you have. You need to link your turns and stop traversing between turns. So your immediate goal is not really to ski faster, but to link your turns. An instructor helps you gain perspective on where to focus your attention, and now can help you add the additional skills to achieve your challenge.

Unfortunately, many of us who have skied a long time have an anthology of horror stories to recount about skiing lessons. We have tales of failure, tyranny, tears, of instructors turning us into puppets. Arms here, legs there, upper body down the hill, knees up the hill.

These days the instructor as Genghis Khan is, we hope, a vanishing species. Many instructors in the United States particularly are paying more attention to communicating with the student, to seeing the student as a whole person and not as a marionette.

But communicating is a two-way street. The student has a responsibility to let the instructor know what she wants, what is happening, and what is the best way for her to get it. You are, in the last analysis, in charge of your own learning. You can't do your part, though, unless you know what you want and what is the best way for you to get it. The first thing to do, if you're planning to take a lesson or a series of lessons, is to assess yourself.

How do you view instructors? As authority figures? How do you react to authority figures? Do you resent being put in a subservient position? Being told what to do? Does the student-teacher relationship bring out all your resistance to parental pressure—do you revert to childhood? Do you feel that being a student is a demeaning role for an adult? Do you feel competitive with the instructor—do you want to show her?

Or do you want to please her? Do you try to "look good" and hide your errors? Do you claim to understand before you really do? Do you apologize every time you make an error?

Don't scold yourself for skiing through class accompanied by a flurry of "I'm sorries." You are only looking for information about yourself. It is information which is potentially more valuable than what you may learn about why you catch an edge.

You know now that you react in a hostile manner to authority. So if an instructor says to you mildly (or authoritatively, for that matter), "Try bending your knees more," you will recognize the rising feelings of rage for what they are—kneejerk reactions. You won't immediately say irritably, "I am bending my knees," or self-pityingly, "I can't bend them any more." You can put the feelings aside and tune in to your knees instead. Can you bend them more? Are they bent? And you can ask without resentment, or without challenge to the instructor, "I think I am bending them. What does it feel like to bend them more?"

We hear many stories of women in tears over lessons. That's because women are more sensitive, more anxious to please, more emotional, say some. But in many cases, those are tears of rage and resentment, not tears of sorrow or hurt feelings. Tears at once again being "pushed around," or trying to live someone else's life, be someone else's person, meet someone else's goals. In this case, it's the instructor's goals, not the husband's or the mother's or the boss's. (The resentment may rise exponentially if the instructor is also husband or mother or boss.)

It is important for us to explore thoroughly, before we go into a lesson, how we perceive our roles as students and how we view instructors. If we do not review our old attitudes and our previous experiences in these terms, we will find ourselves in a lesson that immediately reestablishes patterns of self-punishment and failure. The ogres we have worked so hard to banish—self-consciousness, trying too hard, fear of failure, fear of success—will return.

We are assuming here that you are not taking a Woman's Way seminar where both instructors and students have talked about and discussed these relationships. Even in a Woman's Way seminar, it is amazing and sometimes frustrating to watch how we fall back into the old patterns of waiting for the instructor to comment, praise, and tell us what to do.

Once, in a Woman's Way seminar, Dinah and her class were skiing down the hill thinking about where their weight was—calling out 'Left, left, right, right,' an exercise which had no right or wrong but was used to feed them information about their skiing. Then one by one, the skiers lined up at the bottom of the hill in classic ski school position, waiting tensely for Kathy, their instructor, to come down and tell them whether they had done well or not—and then to tell them what to do next. It was also tempting for Kathy to fall back into the patterns of "detect and correct."

Even when we are all working together, instructor and students, to break those old patterns, it sometimes takes a couple of days. When you are on your own in a standard class situation, it will be up to you and the dialogue you establish with your instructor to banish her as the image of mother or father or second grade teacher.

Set Your Own Goals

It is important to know what *you* want out of a class. Be explicit. If you are taking a ski week, don't just set yourself a vague goal of "I want to ski better."

If you are familiar with the ski area, pick a trail you've never been able to ski with confidence. Say, "I want to ski that solidly from top to bottom." Or "I want to ski this run without a single fall." Or "I want to build my confidence on ice."

Be realistic. Some people set a goal so high, given the length of time they've been skiing and their physical condition, that there's no chance of meeting it. At the start of a ski week, Elissa has heard some students set a mark for the five days that she is still pursuing after twenty-five years of skiing.

Others forget their goals as soon as it becomes obvious they will attain them. They quickly replace one with another. There is no chance for satisfaction.

For instance, one student said, "All I want to do is to be able to make a good parallel turn."

At the end of the day, Elissa remarked, "Well, you made a good parallel turn."

"Oh yes," said the student. "But the snow was so good. Now I want to come down that slope, Heavenly Horror."

Goal-oriented skiers often miss the process of meeting the goal, miss the enjoyment of growth, the changes happening along the way. It's the way someone who's driving from Portland to San Francisco and is thinking only of her goal, of San Francisco, will miss some of the most spectacular scenery in the world by not paying attention to what is happening around her. At the end, San Francisco might not even seem worth the effort of getting there.

When you have decided what your goal is, tell your instructor. Be specific.

It will (1) help your instructor plan where to ski, (2) give some information about your skills or what you think your skills are, (3) tell the rest of the class what you're interested in. It may be that no one else wants to go near ice, in which case you can be directed to another class.

Think about how you learn as we suggested in Chapter 3 (How We Learn to Ski). Are you a watcher? Do you like to ski behind the instructor and try to imitate? A trier? Do you like to have the instructor ski behind you and help you as you ski? Are you an analyzer? A talker? Do you like to verbalize what you're doing or going to do before you translate it into body language? The more you know about what kind of learning situation fits you best, the more likely you are to find it.

Class or Private Lesson?

Should you take a class lesson or a private lesson? A class may be desirable at one time, a private lesson at another. It also depends on what you can afford to pay. Private lessons may run more than $20 an hour; class lessons may cost $6–$10 for an hour and a half. Is it worth the difference? It depends on what you want the lesson to do.

For beginning skiers, class lessons are often the better choice regardless of your bankroll. The other members of the class offer reinforcement and support in what may be perceived as a hostile environment. They are all people of the same skill level, making the same mistakes as you do—falling, getting tangled up in skis and poles, skidding, sliding. You can laugh together and help each other. A group lesson also gives a new skier time to rest between runs as the other skiers go down. There is additional time to groove the new movements and mentally correct them as the instructor is talking or watching the other skiers.

Later on, if you are stuck on a plateau—if, for instance,

your right turns are smooth and solid but your left turns are on the verge of control (most of us are one-legged skiers in one way or another)—an intensive hour with a private instructor may help you work that out. It is much easier to control the environment in a private lesson—what you work on, where you ski, how you interact with the instructor. Private lessons can make a skier feel "safer"; she won't be taken where she doesn't want to ski or asked to do something that she doesn't want to do. On the other hand, some people feel more pressure in a private lesson; they don't like the attention of the teacher focused fully on them, they feel a greater need to please the instructor. Others like the feeling of being special, of "privacy."

If you are clever and do a little preliminary investigating, you may find a way to turn a class lesson into a semiprivate or very small (three or four students) group lesson. If the ski area runs two classes a day, for instance, morning and afternoon, typically the afternoon classes are smaller than the morning ones. At a destination resort, classes on Saturday and Sunday and sometimes even Friday are likely to be very small as the ski-weekers take their last runs and get ready to leave.

Many areas offer what are being called "mountain classes." These are all-day classes with an instructor who serves as combination guide and teacher. Mountain classes cost more than ninety-minute group lessons, but classes may be small. The full day of "guided" skiing may do as much for your skiing and your self-confidence as a week of one-hour lessons.

One turnoff to a class lesson for many people is the traditional ski-off. That is the point at which everyone is shuffling around at the bottom of the teaching hill, hanging around the ski school bell, and you must climb the hill and ski down to demonstrate your best turn so the instructors will know what class to put you in. It is embarrassing and painful—you are isolated on the hill and *everyone* is staring at you. The turn you produce is likely to be awkward and tense, definitely not your best effort. The instructors say,

"Don't worry, we can tell." You may be able to sidestep the ski-off by telling the instructor honestly the best turn you can make or the level of the last class you were in; if this doesn't get you off the hook, just treat the ski-off as information for the instructor. Do not treat it as a test of your worthiness to live. When the lesson starts, ask the instructor to lead off with a relaxing run, rather than an immediate plunge into instruction, so you can shake out the residual tension.

Ski Instructors as Human Beings

It is difficult for many of us to remove the image of the instructor as judge, as arbiter of our lives, as a god. Part of the reason for this is because of the way instructors look. They wear smart uniforms, have shiny new equipment, and are set apart from the rest of the herd on the hill by their health and good looks. You hardly ever see an instructor who's overweight and acned.

This is no coincidence. Often ski instructors are hired not only on the basis of their skiing and/or teaching ability, but on their suitability as a reflection of the area's or the ski school director's image. They wear smart uniforms to support the image, as well as to make it easy to pick them out on the hill.

Because the instructors are thus physically set apart from us ordinary mortals, it is difficult not to put them on a pedestal and attribute to them X-ray perception, good judgment, sterling character, intelligence, and spiritual well-being as well. Sometimes the instructors fall prey to this misconception, too, and think of themselves as special beings. They hang together between lessons, condescend to students, and yes, it is true, occasionally guffaw in the locker room over the "turkey" they have just taught. If they are insecure they will fall back on teaching by the rules, unwilling to experiment, to respond to the students' needs.

Fortunately for both instructor and student, this is a dying breed. (Although it's not dead, yet. When Elissa plugged herself into some cross-country classes as a student, she found instructors who were both condescending and elitist. In another instance, the cross-country class unanimously agreed they just wanted to play, to experiment with what they could learn and experience on their own. They wanted the instructor along as guide and playmate, not teacher. She adamantly refused and insisted on "teaching" the class, giving technical instruction. As Elissa reported, "She robbed us of the experience of just enjoying ourselves.")

Try to forgive the instructors both their uniforms and their good looks. It goes with the job, they can't help it. Try and replace the old image of the instructor as god with the knowledge that this is only a person who knows more about skiing than you do. She or he is not necessarily gifted in any other direction. If the instructor hangs on to her pedestal, try a little imaging. Mentally remove the instructor from the ski slope and put her on your turf. Can she run an employment agency? Juggle home, children, husband, job, and getting everyone to the ski area in time for a lesson? Write a Ph.D. thesis? This is not to abuse the instructor, but to get perspective on a relationship that should not be master-slave, but one of equals exchanging information about each other.

Think about whether you prefer a man or woman as teacher. Sex may not matter if the teacher is openly interested in the student as a whole person, willing to experiment with effective ways of learning. But female role models are important for women in skiing. A woman has a body, capacity for strength, a pattern of movement which women can identify with and imitate. Women instructors were raised with at least some of the same social pressures as their female students.

Male instructors may have difficulty relating to women's physical differences and social patterning. And women may react hostilely to what they perceive as insensitivity.

For example, a young woman was taking a lesson at a western ski area. Her male instructor threw his hip out over his ski and said, "This is how a woman skis."

"How does a sexist ski?" she snapped back.

Not a good beginning for an hour of instruction.

Once you have accumulated all this information about yourself, pass it along to the ski school supervisor or whoever is assigning the instructors: "I'm a beginning parallel skier, but I like to ski fast; I want to work on my parallel turns and make them smoother and faster; I'm more comfortable in a class situation with an instructor who skis a lot and doesn't talk much; I'm still sensitive to criticism, but I like to try new exercises and ideas; I prefer a woman instructor."

This may elicit a stunned "You don't want much, do you" from whoever is making the assignment, but ski schools want their students to be happy. If such a person and such a situation exists in the ski school, you're likely to get it or pretty close to it.

Team Up with the Teacher

You've gone to a great deal of trouble to steer yourself to a good instructor and into a good class situation. How do you now get the most out of it?

You as the student are going to have to work. Learning to ski is now a two-way street. It is not enough to abandon yourself to the instructor and do what she tells you to do as best you can. You have to give her feedback; tell her what you're feeling, what the exercise or maneuver is doing for you, find out what it's intended to do.

A common problem is that instructors tend to verbalize too much, give too many technical directions: "Get forward, push your knee into the hill, rise up on the pole plant."

In an effort to please the instructor, you push your knee into the hill without knowing why, what it is supposed to feel like, or how it relates to the other motions your body is making. Your knee is pleasing the instructor while the rest of your body is in a panic. Ask the instructor how it should "feel"—make her translate the verbal directions to body language. If she is telling you to edge your ski more, ask her how that should feel.

If she's talking about where to hold your poles, take the opportunity to find out where you are actually holding your poles. Forward? Back? Dragging in the snow? What happens when you hold them up? Forward? Back? If you are not happy with the image the instructor is giving you, try your own image. Maybe this is where you hold your arms when you're riding a motorcycle. So ride a motorcycle. But ask the instructor for some feedback on whether you are doing it correctly. Tell her what you've come up with and ask her whether that is what she is trying to do.

If instructors have been prone to verbalize too much, with the advent of new-consciousness ski instruction—those methods of teaching which emphasize body language—emerging now is what Dinah has dubbed the "Mmm School of Ski Instruction." That is the instructor who in her effort not to overdirect, overcriticize, and over-explain goes to the other extreme and says nothing.

"Oh," you say eagerly, anxious to give her feedback, "I'm holding my hands like I'm riding a motorcycle, and I think I'm relaxed but when I plant my pole, I feel my shoulder coming forward. Is that right? Should my upper body be moving too or only my arm?"

"Mmmmmm," says the instructor.

You spend the rest of the ride on the lift trying to decipher whether that "Mmm" was positive or negative, then take another run experimenting with your pole plants. You will undoubtedly eventually discover the position of the arm and the degree of tension that is most comfortable for you, but you will discover nothing from your instructor but that her "Mmm" has a nice vibrato. For that, you could ski with a pitchpipe.

Instructors may, in an effort to squeeze as much as possible into the too-brief class, throw too much at you. They work with edging, then move on to weight-shift and pole plants before the exercise on edging has a chance to groove itself. Elissa, in the process of a tennis lesson, was working happily to perfect tossing the ball for a serve when the instructor called attention to the fact that her racquet was not far enough back. For the moment, that blew both her toss and her swing. Her attention was fragmented; there was too much for her to pay attention to.

If that's happening to you in class, say so. Don't let yourself be rushed. It's better to get one or two things down solidly in the course of a lesson than a half-dozen things vaguely. You need to implant the new movements, to have your muscles memorize them, so that you can recall them tomorrow and not fall victim to amnesia in an hour.

If you learn by watching, then ask for demonstrations again and again until you feel you're imitating correctly. Watch the demonstrations organically, holistically. Don't verbalize mentally what the instructor is doing. Let your body "see" what she is doing, and let your body imitate it. If your body is doing a bad imitation, then ask for some verbal help. Working on pressuring your edges? How does it feel? It feels as if I'm squeezing oranges with my arch; it feels as if I'm collapsing my knee.

In some instances, more dialogue may be useful. As psychologist Virginia Bell says, "Verbal instructions which explain the purpose of a skill and inform the learner what is expected of him appear to have greater value than detailed explanation of skilled movement and the teaching of mechanical principles."

In other words, ask the instructor why you should hold

your poles farther forward or collapse the knee. But unless you're a real bug on biomechanics, it's probably not very useful to get a detailed description of the nerve pathways and physical principles involved in weighting your down-hill ski.

Dinah once spent an entire run during a lesson with Elissa thinking about where her weight was—forward, back, middle—as she thought Elissa had suggested. She had determined that the purpose of the exercise was to help her get her weight forward (she has, over the years, had a lot of lessons in getting her weight forward). As they rode back up the chair lift, Dinah said, "I'm tired of working on getting my weight forward: I'd like to work on my edging for a while." Elissa resisted the temptation to say "Mmm" and said instead, "That's what I was working on." Knowing the goal, that their purposes were the same, changed Dinah's focus. She repeated the exercise but this time with spectacular effect on her edging.

Keep the dialogue alive throughout the lesson.

Instructors sometimes tend to lapse into instructor's jargon. If you don't understand what's being said, ask for a translation or try to translate it yourself and ask if you have understood correctly.

Take Charge of Yourself

Watch for lapses in yourself. You want to please the instructor and make her feel good, so you give her inaccurate feedback—you tell her that you did feel your knee pushing in when in fact what you felt was your shin pushing very hard against your boot.

You don't want to bother the instructor or the class with your inability to grasp a simple explanation, so you let something slip by that is unclear. If you don't understand which is the inside edge of the outside ski, ask. Have the instructor come over and move your ski and leg into position or rephrase the explanation until you do understand. Or get another student to help.

We are often self-conscious about holding up the class, about being the slowest or the dumbest or the clumsiest. So we simply ski along as best we can without asking the questions or experimenting with the new maneuver or exercise. First, focus on what's really happening. Are you the slowest or the dumbest or the clumsiest? Or are you always behind just one or two skiers, and only occasionally behind the rest?

Do you really fall more often or did you just fall on that one run? Aren't other people falling occasionally too?

If you're the only one asking questions, it may be that the others are too shy or too tuned out to do so; your search for information may be helpful to them.

If you're really always far behind everyone else, then maybe you were assigned to the wrong class. Discuss it *then* with the instructor. Maybe there's time for you to join a more appropriate class or drop out of this one and take a rain check on the lesson.

But remember, as one student expressed it, there's a caboose and a locomotive in every class, always a last skier and a first skier. You may enjoy the challenge of being the caboose as much as the responsibility of being the locomotive.

Take charge of your own learning. You don't want to be a puppet; don't ask the instructor to be a puppet master by presenting yourself in class with the attitude, "Here I am. Teach me." She is there to help you, not mold you. If you want her to regard you as a whole person, you must see her as a whole person too.

Instructors worry about their students and their own performances as teachers. They, too, feel pressure; they want to please you. Sometimes, for instance, instructors stop often during a run because they want the student to feel she's getting her money's worth of directions or comment.

Remember also, don't reject your mistakes. If you didn't make mistakes you wouldn't be taking a lesson in the first place. Try to learn from them. Discuss them or focus on them. Fight being discouraged. Classes by their nature are negative because we are concentrating on what we *can't* do, not what we can do. We take what we can do for granted. Review mentally where you started out and what you have accomplished so far. Tune in to the turns that felt good occasionally, not just the ones that felt bad. Be a little easier on yourself. Give yourself some credit for what you have accomplished.

Do give the instructor or the system a chance once you have chosen your class. During Dinah's first Woman's Way seminar, a number of the students ended the first day of skiing with a vaguely unsatisfied feeling. They had had a good time "grunting" and making Z turns vs. S turns and tuning in to their weight, but they grumbled mildly (Dinah among them) that they hadn't really improved their skiing much. Trust us, the instructors said wisely. The students did, and by the end of the second day, not only were they still having fun on skis, but their skiing had improved visibly.

7

Technique:
The Rules of the Game

"If you're going to write about technique," said Gloria, a Woman's Way student, "please don't use any diagrams. I never could get anything out of all those little feet running around the pages of ski magazines."

There won't be any little feet, but we do want to talk about the way Woman's Way teaches skiing and the kind of skiing it teaches.

This is not a chapter on "How to ski"; dozens of books have been devoted to that subject. In any case, we don't think you can learn to ski from a book with or without little feet. We do believe, however, that if you know what ski technique is aiming for, why boots and skis are designed the way they are, why the learning progression of most ski instruction is designed the way it is, the why of all the exercises, on bending the ankles and knees, feeling your edges, side-slipping, then you will learn more quickly and enjoy the learning process more.

Technique is a subject that sends a lot of skiers onto automatic pilot. Mention a term like down-unweighting, and they immediately push a button that locks an alert expression on their faces, while their thoughts flee to the pleasures of a hot tub.

That most discussions of ski technique, either on the hill or in ski literature, quickly degenerate into jargon is usually the fault of the speaker or writer. It is why a lot of people quickly turn off when terms like down-unweighting vs. up-unweighting, foot-swiveling vs. carving creep into the conversation. That theoreticians do not present technique well should not lead us to reject what they are trying to say. We should insist instead that they try harder to make it clear.

Skiing is a complex motor skill which requires an extraordinary amount of bodily coordination. Some of it involves movements that are totally foreign to our muscles. The skier also grapples with strong natural forces like gravity, inertia, and centrifugal force. We denigrate ourselves and what we are doing or trying to do if we shrug off attempts at analysis as irrelevant or pretentious. Women more than men may have a tendency to belittle themselves and their accomplishments—and the sport—by dodging discussion of technique.

It may not be easy for a weekend skier to understand why some turns are better than others, why some stances on skis are better than others, or why she should bother. But trying to understand can make skiing more meaningful and help us be better skiers. It is worth the effort.

Why is it worth the effort? Why don't we just get out there, after we have shed our fears and uncertainties, and ski the best way we can? For a number of reasons. One, that is reinventing the wheel. There are already hundreds of skiers who have gone before and who have thought about it, analyzed it, and are able to talk about and teach shortcuts to "the best way we can." Why not take advantage of what they have already learned, just as we use a cookbook or a preprogrammed computer?

Two, learning theorists believe that we learn better and

more quickly if we know what our goals are and what the aim or purpose of each step to the goal is.

Three, if we are to get the most from our skiing in terms of creativity, self-expression, challenge, and pleasure, anarchy simply won't do. We have chosen the game we wish to play and in order to play it well—to be able to concentrate, to focus—we must play it within the rules.

Who makes the rules and why should we follow them? We do, in all games, even in skiing. And the rules follow a logical sequence only in terms of an arbitrary goal. Why is tennis played on a rectangular court marked off with lines and a net across the middle? Because we say so; we have agreed—or at least tennis players have agreed—that that is the field upon which the game will be played. All the rules involving the ball in play, scoring and technique follow with some logic from the basic, albeit arbitrary, parameters of the game. Two people can get out on a tennis court and agree to simply bash the ball around, hitting it whenever they can no matter how often the ball bounces and whether it falls within the bounds of the court or not. They are playing a game, indeed, a game they may enjoy, but they are not playing "tennis" as we have defined it.

Playing games or sports within the accepted rules is analogous to the structure of an art form. Within the artistic structure, self-expression and creativity take place. If you choose to paint you are already limited in expression by the medium you have chosen. You may work in oils or acrylics, you may paint upon a canvas or upon a California hillside, but you are painting—you are not dancing, sculpting, or composing music.

As soon as you choose to ski rather than ice skate or bobsled or build ice sculptures, you have chosen a structure within which to play. You have accepted the limitations of that structure. Within that structure, you may strive for mastery of the subtle movements required, of the equipment, of the "playing field"—the mountain and the snow—and ultimately mastery of your body and yourself.

By accepting the limits of the sport, you are providing for yourself an almost unlimited opportunity to experiment with your ability to grow, to change, to create, to role play, to discover yourself. Because you are contained safely within the game, because the rules of the game have been clearly established beforehand, your energies can be directed to exploring the opportunities for creative growth within that structure.

It is important to understand that what we are doing in skiing—the limits which we accept and set—and the way we do it is by consensus only. There is no Olympian power dictating how or which way to ski. You will not be struck by Zeus's thunderbolts if you choose not to play the game. If you do not like the kind of turns Woman's Way teaches, learn to make another kind of turn. You are in control.

Knowing that gives perspective to the sport. If a controlled turn is what today's skiers agree is the goal, and you choose to spend the rest of your days in an uncontrolled wedge, then you are only playing a different game. You are not committing a capital crime. Of course, your choice may bring with it certain consequences. Other skiers may be reluctant to play with you. You may be unable to ski fast and to ski certain kinds of terrain, but it is still your choice. There is no inherent "wrong," no immorality involved.

Let's Take Turns

There is an old joke among ski writers that there are only two articles about skiing that have ever been written or will be written, "How to Turn" and "Turns I Have Made." Everything else is a variation on those themes. As is often the case in long-lived jokes, there is Great Truth. For most of us, everything we do in skiing from the moment we struggle with our first set of bindings is directed to learning to turn. We turn to decrease our speed, to guide us into a better line on the mountain, to find the best snow, to avoid obstacles, to stop. Eventually, turning becomes a pleasure in itself.

There are all kinds of ways to turn our skis, ranging from the very old and very beautiful Telemark turn, rapidly returning to vogue among cross-country skiers, to winding the upper body in the direction of the turn in the hope that the skis will obey one of the laws of motion and follow. There is foot-swiveling, hopping, even stepping around a turn.

We repeat; Make the kind of turn that makes you happy, secure, comfortable. We repeat this because this perspective sometimes gets lost in a blizzard of invective when ski technicians get together. There are those who think their way of making a turn is the only way, those who believe that the old way or the new way or the Tasmanian way is the "right" way. But the rapid changes in equipment technology, in the care of ski slopes and the new methods of teaching virtually insure that there is no "right" way, and even if there were, it won't stay right for long.

Still, you have to make a turn somehow. The kind of turn that is widely accepted these days and that Woman's Way has adopted is called a "carved" turn. It is dedicated to economy of motion. Skiing with economy of motion means getting the most out of our equipment and using the equipment to its full potential. It means letting the skis and boots and the mountain do most of the work. It is a game which Elissa believes gives us the most options with the least effort.

She says, "Sometimes I like to ski fast and sometimes I don't. Sometimes I challenge myself to ski difficult conditions and terrain and sometimes I don't. I don't even care especially whether or not I am a 'pretty' skier, although I assume that the more efficiently I use my equipment, the better I will look to those who understand my game. But whether I am skiing fast or slow, on difficult terrain or not, it is the precision with which I make my turns that absorbs me."

This sensitivity to the way we control skis in a turn also helps us stay on top of rapid equipment changes.

In a perfect carved turn, the edges of the skis literally carve a little banked arc in the snow against which the skis ride just like a bobsled rides against the bank of a turn on the slide. Once a perfect carved turn is started, if it could complete its course with no interference from gravity or change in slope, snow, or pressure, it would make a perfect circle.

The carved turn makes the maximum use of ski equipment as it is designed today. It lets the ski do the work. Here is how. Put a standard recreational ski flat on the ground or on the snow and look at it from the top. You will notice it has a "waist." The middle of the ski is narrower than the tip or the tail of the ski. This is called the side cut. Some skis will have virtually no side cut at all. These are beginner or freestyle skis and are for limited use. Some will have a "waist" like Scarlett O'Hara. These are racing skis. The side cut makes it easy to initiate the turn and to control its arc when the ski is in reverse camber.

What, you may well ask, is reverse camber. Camber is another characteristic built into modern skis. If you get down on the floor and look at your flat ski from the side, you will notice that in the area of the waist the ski arches slightly above the floor, like the arch of a foot. If you push down on the ski with your hand, it will flatten out and meet the floor, making a flat ski. Take your hand away and it will spring back into an arch. This is camber. It serves to distribute a skier's weight along the full length of the ski, so that when you stand on your skis, the tip and tail are bearing some of the burden.

If you suspend the ski between two chairs and push very hard, the ski will go into reverse camber. It will arch in the opposite direction with the tip and tail up, the center depressed. You have begun to make a circle with your skis.

The harder you push, the smaller will be the radius of the circle.

When you are on skis, ready to make a turn, you tip the ski onto its edge. Apply pressure to the edge and it will begin to dig into the snow and carve a turn. The more pressure that is put on the edge, the more it is pushed into reverse camber, the smaller will be the radius of the turn. It is the ski (and gravity and centrifugal force) that is doing most of the work. All you have to do is stay balanced over the ski, keep it on edge, and adjust the pressure and the ski will do the turning. The feeling is like what one of the Woman's Way students called "front wheel drive." The ski is pulling you around the turn.

Carved turns require less energy, they are more economical of motion, because there is less movement of the body. Beginning and even intermediate skiers tend to think that it is the upper body that controls the turn. We throw our hips in the direction we want to go as if we were doing the conga. More expert and more experienced skiers learn that legs and feet and the position of the skis can control the turn. The upper body can stay quiet, moving only enough to finesse balance and pressure on the skis.

Skidded turns, turns where the tails of the skis are skidded around to complete the turn, not only require more energy to initiate, but maintaining stability and control is more difficult. While you may have deliberately started the skid, once the skis begin to slide, you are no longer really in control. The upper body bobs and weaves to maintain a balanced position over the skis. Warren Witherell, in *How the Racers Ski,* compares the difference between a skidded turn and a carved turn with the difference between turning a bicycle on a wet pavement and on a dry pavement. When the street is wet, the bicycle has a tendency to slip out from under you; so does a ski on a skidded turn.

Because women seem to be more concerned than men with getting it "right," with mastering the subtleties of technique and equipment to make their turns—perhaps because they don't rely on an ability to muscle their way through a turn—the finesse and sensitivity needed to master and control a carved turn makes it an ideal technique for women.

You Can't Always Carve

Having touted the rewards of a carved turn, it is now time to say that a pure carved turn is rare. Usually, for an ordinary recreational skier, even an expert, it is impractical and sometimes impossible, to carve a turn all the way through.

It is impractical when the radius of the turn you want to make is smaller than the radius of the ski if pushed into maximum reverse camber. To make a short-radius turn, you have to steer the turn a bit to start it around. Steering is actively guiding the ski in the direction you want to go, usually by turning the skis with your feet or legs. You can also use movement of the shoulders or hips (as many women do) to turn the skis, but the skis will probably overturn. You will either be traversing when you don't want to be or in the position of having to make another hard, fast, oversteered turn all the while you are fighting for balance.

Once the short-radius turn is started, then you can use the edge and pressure to finish in a carve.

The initial steering action will probably cause the tails to skid a little. Sometimes you want the skis to skid a little, because you want to slow down. You release the edge and slip sideways a bit to wipe off some speed when, for instance, you are skiing a difficult mogul field.

Sometimes the skier is not physically strong enough to hold a carved turn. When you are going fast and carving your turns, a good deal of centrifugal force builds up against the ski edge. The faster you go, the more force is pushing against the ski. It takes quite a bit of strength to keep the ski from being pushed sideways, to hold the edge in the snow.

It's also hard to hold an edge if the snow is very hard or if the slope is very steep. To carve a turn under every circumstance usually requires more strength than the average recreational skier has. It also requires sensitivity and awareness of the snow and the body. Besides being able to hold the edge against forces tending to flatten or push the skis, the pressure and the amount of edging must be adjusted as different textures of snow are encountered in the course of a turn. Sometimes you actually have to steer away from the direction of your intended turn to keep from overturning.

"Carving" not only demands strength and sensitivity, it also requires a great deal of skill. Carving is put in quotes because a carved turn is only relatively carved. Not only is it at times impractical, sometimes impossible, to carve every turn totally, but skis are not truly designed to carve.

Despite side cut and camber, the tip or shovel of the ski is still the widest part of the ski. Therefore, the tip of the ski will bite more deeply into the snow than the tail. More friction is created at the front than at the rear of the ski, and as we turn, the tails will tend to skid. The slight skid will help bring the skis around faster; the carving action will help control the arc of the turn. More pressure forward or backward (called leverage) will also affect the skis' behavior, the size of the arc, and the relative amount of carving and sliding.

The turn that has the least skid and the most carve is what we are striving for. But with all these factors—amount of edging, amount of pressure under the foot, adjustments of balance to compensate for skis and changes in terrain—it is no wonder that most of us never achieve, may not even want to achieve, that perfect series of carved turns.

We have not even begun to introduce the subject of arm movement, which also affects what is happening to our turns. Just as natural forces and laws are working on our skis, so do they work on our upper bodies. "For every action there is an equal and opposite reaction" is operative here. If you move your arm forward, the center of balance and the quality of the pressure on your skis will change. To stay in balance and to continue doing what you want to do, you must adjust skis, legs, body, perhaps only minutely, but adjust nonetheless.

It's easy to understand why a sense of balance is almost as critical to a skier as it is to a tightrope walker. Why being able to tune in to your body, to understand where it is and what it can do, and to make the minute adjustments necessary is crucial to skiing.

We Learn One Octave at a Time

How can we deal with all that—edging, pressuring, balance, skidding, not skidding. That's too much to think about, particularly if you're sliding downhill. That's right. It is too much to think about. So we learn to do it without thinking about it. We learn and practice each new skill until it becomes automatic and no longer enters into our conscious thought. And we don't do it all at once. Skiing is a complicated, a very complicated, compendium of motor skills; no one acquires them all at once. We all learn to ski in stages.

The basic sequence of learning to ski, as Woman's Way teaches it, goes something like this.

1. Learn to stand, walk, climb, go straight down a little incline—basically get used to the feeling of your skis. Explore positions of balance on the moving ski. Learn to stop with a wedge (ski tips pointed at each other).

2. Beginning turn, a wedge turn. Learning to steer one leg—the outside leg (downhill leg at the end of the turn). In a wedge, one ski is already in the direction you want to go and you use that ski to steer the turn. The other ski—the inside ski—is controlled just enough to keep it out of the way, as you begin to steer, edge and put pressure on the outside ski.

3. Refining the turn into a wedge christie. Still steering with the outside leg to start the turn (it is easier to handle a turn one leg at a time at first), match the inside ski (bring it parallel) to help smooth and finish the turn. Tune in to the sensations in the knee and foot of that inside leg as you pivot it. Continue working on edging the skis and putting pressure on them. The skis begin to skid a little at the end of the turn. Work on balance at a little faster speed and balancing on a skidding ski.

4. More refining into parallel turns—turning both skis at the same time. Still turning and steering the skis, begin to use edging and pressuring as turning devices instead of pushing them around. Put pressure on the outside ski earlier in the turn.

5. Continue refining and consolidating edging, pressuring skills. Work on balance on various types of terrain, snow, different types of turns (short-radius, long-radius, skidding; more carving, less skidding).

6. Keep practicing refining, linking parallel turns, play with speed, terrain, all types of snow.

7. Keep playing, enjoying, learning more and more to trust your body, your equipment, your feet and legs to do what they should do.

Some ski teachers would skip the wedge turn altogether since it's quickly abandoned. But most instructors—and most skiers—feel it's not only a useful turn (even experts use it occasionally), but it gives beginners the security they need to feel comfortable on the snow and to be able to enjoy the downhill run immediately.

Not every ski school, instructor, or skier has the carved

turn as the ultimate goal but the relationship of steps in sequence is still the same, as it is in every complex skill. You begin to play the piano with only one hand at a time using only one octave. You add an octave and play with both hands at once and so forth. There are exercises in piano playing to improve hand strength, coordination, to fine-tune your ear, to explore the possibilities of what can be done on the instrument. There are also exercises in skiing that serve the same purpose—sideslipping, bouncing, numbering knee bends. The goal is to gain control of both the instruments and yourself. Once that is accomplished, you choose the sonatas you wish to play; you choose the slope or the snow or the speed at which you wish to go.

Once you have learned the rules and acquired the skills to play the game of skiing, you are free to choose when and where and how you want to play it. You may devote yourself to what Lito Tejada-Flores of Squaw Valley calls "adventure terrain," always seeking a challenge; you may specialize in "pleasure terrain," refining and building skills, simply enjoying what you can do. You can change every day, one day seeking speed, another experimenting with different techniques or turns or tricks, another simply trying to survive the weather. You can express yourself to the fullest.

However, before you start expressing yourself from the top of an Alp after you have made your first parallel turn, it's important to be realistic about how much progress you can make and exactly what you can take on. While it may be true that anyone can learn to ski, it is not true that everyone can learn to ski equally well. What is relevant in terms of how much progress you can make and how quickly you make it is not only your previous athletic experience and any kind of innate athletic ability (good reflexes, good balance) you may or may not have, but your physical condition and exactly how much time you can or want to devote to skiing. Remember, as you learn to ski like Cindy Nelson or your instructor, that racers and freestylers and instructors train and ski *every* day, some of them all day.

To make a carved turn takes strength and skill, to master all kinds of terrain and snow conditions takes constant practice. If you are a weekend skier, as most of us are, don't demand too much of yourself. Don't be discouraged if your ski tracks look like someone is following you with a push broom because you're skidding all your turns. It takes a long time to get there, so enjoy the journey. Who knows what adventures and pleasures you'll have along the way.

8

Ski Tips for Women Only

No matter what kinds of turns we make—carved, skidded, wedge—chances are we do not make them exactly like a man. There are physical differences between men and women—no snickers, please—and therefore differences in how men and women move and stand on skis. There are differences in center of gravity, distribution of body mass, potential maximum strength of arm and shoulders, and looseness of joints. Even where theoretically women could be as strong as men, in the leg, for instance, they usually are not because of differences in athletic history and conditioning.

While much of the material in this book would be useful to men—they too suffer from performance pressure and could find relief in breathing, centering, tuning in, etc.— this chapter is addressed to the most common problem women have on skis as a result of their anatomy. These exercises can help women take advantage of the differences in anatomy, help them be more effective on skis. They are not designed to make a woman ski like a man or look like a man on skis. Try them and you will still ski like a woman, only better.

Not every woman needs every exercise in this chapter. For instance, many women are knock-kneed. It has to do with the way the thighbone's connected to the hipbone. But there are plenty of women whose legs are perfectly straight, and some who are bowlegged. There are also knock-kneed women who ski happily without special help. However, if you are knock-kneed and that condition causes you to ride on the inside edges of your skis, prevents you from flattening the inside ski on a turn, or causes your knees to hit each other and block each other when they are trying to edge, then read the section on knock-knees.

Tune In to Where the Weight Is

A man's muscle mass is concentrated in his chest, shoulders, and upper arms, with relatively flat buttocks and slim pelvis. Most women have more mass at their hips, with full buttocks and thighs, in addition to a wider pelvis. These differences generate differences in the relative positions in which men and women find their optimum balance on skis.

In skiing, there is a constant need to keep the body forward over the moving, accelerating skis. When we move our body forward a little—flex a little at the hip, knee, and ankle—the upper body is over the balls of the feet. For many men, this is ideal—it puts the bulk of the weight where it belongs. For many women, however, the bulk of the weight is still over her heels. If this is the case, she must make an additional effort to get her weight farther forward.

One way to do this is to play with the leverage exercises in Chapter 5 (What to Do About It). Tune in to the way different parts of the foot feel when the weight is forward, middle, or back. Tune in to the feeling of pressure produced by the boot on the front of the ankle—a lot of pressure, little pressure, no pressure.

More advanced skiers can tune in to dramatic weight changes in a turn by lifting the tip of the inside ski, lifting the whole inside ski, lifting the tail of the inside ski.

Other things to try:

Ride a bicycle. Try this experiment on skis. Stand still and hold your arms forward as if you were riding a bicycle (the old-fashioned kind, not the ten-speed racer kind). Now drop them slowly. Feel the weight move from the front of the foot to the heel. Raise your arms again slowly. Feel your weight move forward again. The feeling in your feet will tell you the optimum place to hold your arms as you ski. In general, when they drop out of sight, when you can't see them from the corners of your eyes, your weight is being pulled back. Bringing them forward—remembering to ride the bicycle—will bring the weight forward.

Bounce against the front of your boot. Push yourself against the front of your boot and let the top of the boot bounce you back. Bounce forward again. Feel the difference in pressure against the front of your ankle as you do this. Feel the different points of pressure underfoot. Practice that exercise a few times, bouncing down the hill, and you'll develop a good sense of where your body is when it is forward.

Pull your ski back (if you can do a wedge christie or more advanced turn). Instead of trying to put your body forward, pull your outside ski, your steering ski, back under your hips as you are completing a turn. This puts you in a good balanced position of control over your ski. If you get the feeling that your skis are always getting away from you—that they are going out of control—try this exercise.

Flex the ankle. In general, jokes about "bending zee knees" to the contrary, it is not the lack of bend in the knees that causes a skier to be back on her skis as much as it is lack of bend in her ankles. Amount of ankle bend is one of the characteristics distinguishing a pretty good skier from a very good skier.

Try this: holding on to something for support, bend your knees without bending your ankles. This puts you in a sitting position (what some skiers call an "outhouse crouch") or back and out of balance. Now flex your ankles as well as your knees (letting your torso flex from the hips a little as well) as if you were going to leap into the air. You should feel balanced over your feet. This, basically, is the position we want to be in on our skis. Of course, we are moving on our skis, which means constant adjustments to remain in that position of balance.

One of the hindrances to this athletic, balanced stance is our ski boots. The fact that our ski boots are rigid and high allows us to transmit the messages of our legs and knees to the skis. It also helps us to keep from falling when we get off-balance. However, the height and rigidity of the boots does interfere with our ability to flex our ankles. The boot has to be stiff enough so that it does its work, but if you find that you are always back on your heels, that you cannot get forward, you might want to loosen your top buckle. You can even open it altogether if that doesn't cause a great sacrifice in control. Or consider getting a different pair of boots.

Straighten up. In their effort to get forward, many people bend too much at the waist. It does no good to tell yourself to stop bending from the waist. Straighten up and most likely you will fall on your gluteus maximus. Your body is too smart to let you do that. Before you change that bend at the waist, make the other changes that get you forward. Then perhaps your wise body will straighten up on its own.

There is also such a thing as being too far forward. When you are, the tails of your skis will slide out.

With all of these exercises keep in mind that there is no

set "position" on skis that is desirable for every ski, in every snow condition, on every slope. We are experimenting to find out what it feels like to be balanced; the position in which we are most stable will vary with each turn, each dip in terrain, each new piece of equipment—remember Holly, our racer in Chapter 3. Keep your options open.

Loose as a Goose

Women do generally seem to have a looser ligamentous structure than men. That is, women have tendons, ligaments, and connecting and supporting tissues that are more flexible and more resilient than men's.

A woman, for instance, can scratch her own back or pull up a back zipper because her shoulder, elbow, and wrist joints are looser than a man's. She can bend, flex, rotate, and contort herself into positions that are difficult if not impossible for most men. This is wonderful if you're a dancer or your back itches a lot. It demands some consideration in skiing. Because of the relative looseness of her knee joints, it may take a woman fractionally longer than a man to edge her skis. Also a woman usually has to angulate more than a man. That is, she usually has to push her knees, or knees and hips, toward the hill more than a man does to experience the same amount of edging. Her looser joints will absorb some of the movement before it is transmitted to the ski.

(This is one of the reasons why it is good for women to pattern themselves after good women skiers—to watch demonstrations given by women, to image or visualize a woman when they are practicing visualization, and to ask women how it feels to perform a particular movement.)

Many women, in the effort to get their ski on edge, angulate primarily with their hips. Hip angulation is useful and even necessary, especially at higher speeds. But in short turns, it takes longer to move the ski from edge to edge. It takes less time to transmit the message to the skis and less side-to-side movement if edging is directed from the knees rather than from the hips.

What is more, too much angulation from the hip will sometimes cause the weight to go onto the uphill ski. Try this: with your side turned toward a wall and your hand against it for balance, move your hips slowly toward the wall, keeping your feet in place. You will feel your feet go onto their edges. Keep moving your hip to the wall, however, and you should feel a shift of weight to the foot closest to the wall. When you're skiing, of course, centrifugal force offsets this weight shift. However, particularly if you are not going very fast, pushing your hip too much into the hill may put your weight where you don't want it to be.

Here are some exercises to help a skier add knee action to hip action:

Take a slightly wider stance. If feet and knees are locked together, as in the pretty pictures, it is difficult to use the knees to edge effectively; they tend to bang into each other. Keep the feet far enough apart so that you can use each knee independently, so that one knee won't bang into the other. Then you won't be thrown back to your hips for effective edging.

Sensitizing the controls. Try pressing the arch of the outside foot into the snow, as though you wanted to flatten it. At the initiation of the turn the pressure under the arch is fairly light; as the turn continues, it increases. It is as if you were squeezing oranges under your arch. Next get the feeling of pressing your ankle against the inside of the ski boot, pushing it toward the snow. First try this standing still in order to identify the sensations involved—where you feel pressure from the boot, how the knee feels as it too is pushed in.

Corraling the calf (for parallel skiers). As you complete a turn, push the outside knee toward the calf of the inside leg. Try it on dry land first. Actually try to get one knee down toward the calf, *not tucked behind the other knee.* Your skis will have to be somewhat apart to do this. Feel what that does to the edges of your skis.

The edged wedge. On relatively smooth, easy terrain we can use our old friend the wedge to help us explore edging (and to explore pressure forward and backward on our skis). Take a wedge position and start moving directly down the fall line. Choose terrain on which you are comfortable but not a slope so flat that you are barely moving. After you have built up a little speed, put *one* ski on edge. Now put pressure on it by trying to flatten your arch and push the inside of your ankle against your boot. The ski, riding on its edge, will make a turn. Don't *try* to make a turn. The turn will result from what your arch, ankle, and the edge of your ski are doing. After a few seconds let up on that ski. Put the other ski on edge and push the arch and ankle of the other foot toward the snow. Alternate down the fall line. Remaining in the wedge will give you security and keep your speed down. Later those same sensations can be transferred to your parallel turns.

Daughter of edged wedge. Warren Witherell, in *How the Racers Ski,* suggests this one. Again, pick a moderate slope so you won't pick up too much speed. Ski with your skis parallel and about two feet apart. Keep the skis flat, but now put most of your weight on your right ski. Now move only your right knee to the inside, putting your right ski on its inside edge. Don't bend your hip, don't slide the tail of your ski, don't try to turn. Just edge your ski with your knee and push the arch and ankle into the snow. You will make a long carved turn. Release the edge (move the knee back), shift most of your weight to the left ski, and do the same with your left knee, arch, and ankle. You'll make a long carved turn to the right. Your other ski—the unedged ski—will follow along nicely.

Keep using your knees and pressure on your arch and ankles as you make a series of turns. Use this exercise also to experiment with what happens when you move pressure forward and back on the foot.

The flasher. Pretend there is someone standing downhill from you. As you come out of the fall line in your turn, flash the base of your ski to her so she can read the writing on the bottom. Do it both ways.

Think skis, not body. Some women get their bodies into perfect positions of beautiful angulation, but their skis remain virtually flat on the snow. We want the skis on edge; body movement (angulation of the hip, knee, ankle, and inclination of the whole body toward the center of the turn) just helps to get them there. We are not posing for a skiing sculpture; we want to move as efficiently as possible. If you focus on your skis and whether they are on edge or not, then your body will make the minimum amount of movement to get them there. When you are edging appropriately for the speed and radius of the turn, it feels as if you are bracing against the edge.

Weakness in Arms and Shoulders

Women seem to be relatively weaker in the arms and shoulders than men. This won't affect most skiing maneuvers since strength is needed in the legs, not the arms and shoulders. However, many women find it extremely difficult to get up after a fall by the standard method of pulling themselves up with their poles, which does demand arm and shoulder strength. Also a woman's body mass is farther away from point of leverage than a man's, thus demanding more lift. Here are two ways to get up after a fall that put less demand on arm strength.

The herringbone lift. You've fallen and are gracelessly sprawled in the snow. Untangle skis and poles. Roll over on your stomach with your head uphill, your knees bent and your skis in the air. Lower your skis to form a V with the tails close together and the tips spread apart. This is the same position you use for walking up the hill with a herringbone step. With both poles in one hand push yourself up on your knees, "walking" your hands downhill toward your knees until you are able to push yourself to your feet. If necessary, use a pole in each hand for the last few inches of lift. You are now standing, facing uphill with your skis forming a V. Using your poles, step around until your skis are parallel and facing across the hill. You're ready to begin skiing again.

The stem lift. It helps with this one if you open the top buckles of your boots. Get into the standard transitional position for picking yourself up—skis parallel and across the fall line, body uphill of your skis, pole straps off your wrists and both poles in your uphill hand. Bring your feet relatively close to your buttocks, put your uphill hand above the baskets of both poles, your downhill hand on the tops of both poles. Plant both poles near your uphill thigh. Now move your downhill ski back so that its tail is pointed somewhat up the hill behind the other and its tip is pointed somewhat downhill. This will automatically put your torso in a more forward position. As you push down on your poles, roll forward and onto your downhill knee. Rest. Then roll forward and up onto your uphill ski. Remember to keep rolling forward as you rise.

Knock-knees ================================

Because of a woman's wider pelvis, the femur or long thighbone joins the pelvis at a different angle from that in a man. For many women this results in knock-knees. This is the proper way for women to be put together and creates no problems in walking, standing, and other daily activities, or even most sports. However, skiing is basically unnatural behavior, and the combination of rigid ski boots plus the kinds of maneuvers necessary to create turns may exaggerate a woman's knock-kneed stance, causing ski instructors to make bad jokes and women to be self-conscious. Ignore the jokes—knock-knees are a difference, not a liability. Try these exercises to keep your knees from knocking:

Anticipate with the inside knee. Knock-knees often cause a skier to stand more on the inside edges of the skis when she pushes her knees forward. It is easy for her to get onto the new turning edge (the inside edge of the outside ski) but more difficult to flatten the inside ski. Thus, the inside ski is stemmed more or longer than she wants; she may even be forced to lift it to release the edge. A way to correct that is to start the turn by moving what will be the inside knee (it's the downhill knee as the new turn starts) in the intended direction of the turn a split second before starting the other turning movements. This will release the edge, flatten the ski, and allow the turn to proceed smoothly.

Take a wide stance. If you must tuck one knee behind the other to initiate your turns effectively, or if you feel one knee pressing against the other when you are edging, try keeping your skis a little farther apart. If a skier is knock-kneed and tries to ski with legs and feet close together, the knees may get in each other's way like Tweedledum and Tweedledee. Move legs and feet farther apart and the knees are free to move from side to side as you change edges.

The stem-step turn. This is a particularly easy turn for a knock-kneed woman to do because she can get onto her new edge quickly. It also makes it easier to start that first turn, helps reduce skidding on hard snow, and aids in carving.

To do the stem-step turn: from a traverse position, *step* the uphill ski out onto its downhill edge, pointing the tip somewhat downhill. Transfer your weight onto it, putting pressure forcefully on the edge. As you feel the edge bite and begin to pull you through the turn (front-wheel drive, remember) draw the inside ski parallel.

Pelvic rock. Many women stand on skis with their backs arched, in a swayback position. This makes the thighs rotate inward, producing a knock-kneed, pigeon-toed stance. It also reduces the mobility of the hip joint. To correct this, put your pelvis, not your abdomen, in the lead. Bring the pelvis forward and think of it as leading the way down the hill. Or imagine a beam of light emanating from your center and lighting your way down the hill, as we described in Chapter 5 (What to Do About It). Your back will straighten, your hip will unlock, and you'll be able to ski more fluidly.

If you continue to have trouble with your edging as a result of knock-knees, you should consider trying cants, boots with built-in wedges, or orthotics (see Chapter 9, Equipment: The Tools of the Game). For some women that is an excellent—and maybe the only—solution.

Other Useful Exercises

Block that hip. All skiers are tempted to use their bodies to power or boost the start of a turn. Women tend to call upon their hips to emphasize transfer of weight from one ski to another, or grind one hip around to start a turn. But throwing a hip over the outside ski (the turning ski) tends to flatten it, preventing it from edging properly. At the same time the inside ski is put on edge. This is exactly the opposite of what we want to make an effective turn: The outside ski should be on its inside edge; the inside ski should be flat so we can start the turn. The feeling, when everything is going right, is that pressure is being transmitted directly from the outside hip, through the leg, to the holding edge.

If the hips are what we are using to shift our weight and to turn our skis, we cannot stop doing it until we have found something else that works. We cannot stop using our hips until we start using our legs.

Experiment again with the edged wedge exercise. This time tune in to your hips. Are they moving from side to side? Are they powering the turn? Just be conscious of what you are doing; don't try to change it. Once you have felt yourself turning a hip, it is much easier to do something about it.

Try the wide-track position (Daughter of Edged Wedge). Really bend ankles and knees—a 4 or so in our number game. It is much easier to use the legs to turn when they are bent. Make some turns now, steering strongly with both legs. Once you have become familiar with the sensations involved, it is easier to integrate them into your skiing.

The edging exercises above will help you be aware of using your legs more effectively.

The knee-to-calf exercise for parallel skiers ("corraling the calf") will not only help you to use your edges more effectively but help bring your hips under control. Try it on dry land and see how it not only puts the foot or ski on edge, but also what happens to the hips. They are pushed into the hill, but they are also rotated in the opposite direction of the turn.

Reudi Baer, in *Pianta Su*, stresses the importance of

keeping the hips from facing across the hill at the end of the turn. He suggests that the parallel skier should make a conscious effort at the end of the turn to rotate the hips away from the direction of the turn to some degree. The hips are then anticipating the next change in direction.

When do you shift weight? One of the earmarks of a precisely executed turn is an early transfer of weight to the new outside ski. The expert skier steps onto her new outside ski at the initiation of the turn or even at the completion of the old turn. Pay attention to the point at which you are transferring your weight. Tune in to it exactly. When you have done so, on the next turn make the transfer just a fraction earlier.

Timing pole plants. Watch a good skier. Every time her pole tip touches the snow say "tip"; when her turn starts, say "turn." Get the rhythm "tip, turn, tip, turn." Now you start out, but keep the same rhythm; as you say "tip," touch the tip of your pole to the snow; as you say "turn," start your turn.

Rhythm. Set a rhythm for your turns before you begin your run. Hum a tune with a strong beat, disco, perhaps, and turn on every beat. Or say some nonsense syllable to yourself rhythmically, "dum, dum, dum" like a drumbeat, and turn whenever you say the word. You decide before you start off what the rhythm will be, fast or slow, and so you decide what the spacing of the turns will be.

Exploring Aggressiveness ▬▬▬▬▬▬

Some women feel they need to be more "aggressive" on skis, to ski faster and link turns closer together. Here are two exercises to explore aggressiveness.

Go, go, go. This exercise is related to the one above, in which you predetermine your rhythm for the run. This time, however, use the words "go, go, go." Before you start your run decide how fast, loud, and driving the "go's" will be. Ski down a slope saying the "go's" out loud and assertively. Turn on every "go." Increase the rhythm of the "go, go"; decrease it. How does this affect your turns? Your confidence? Say it out loud so you'll pay attention to yourself. If you say it mentally, you are likely to be distracted more easily.

Rate the aggressiveness of your run. As you ski, give your aggressiveness a rating of from 1 (for least aggressiveness) to 5 (most aggressive). As with other rating exercises, in the beginning don't try to change your aggressiveness, just rate it. In the next run, do a series of turns which you've rated 1; now do a series which you've rated 5. Try 2s, 3s, 4s. What difference does that make in your skiing; at what level are you comfortable?

Raising Your Carving Consciousness

To become more aware of the differences between a carved turn and a sliding turn, try this exercise. Make Z's in the snow; slide each turn so that you are inscribing the sharp-angled letter Z in the snow. Really exaggerate the Z, so that the slope is etched with the mark of Zorro. Now make S's in the snow. Concentrate on linking the soft half-circles of an S; say to yourself S-s-s-s-s so that you're reinforced by the slithering sound. Think about the differences; how did the Z feel; how did the S feel? (One student responded straight-faced, "Like we were making S's of ourselves.") What was your body doing to make the difference?

An afternoon spent doing these exercises would not be an afternoon of unmitigated joy. These exercises are intended to be practiced only occasionally when there is a particular problem that demands your attention. They are designed to sensitize you to other ways of moving and standing on skis. Don't get caught up in perfecting Z's and S's for instance. Beware of perfectionism, beware of performance pressure, beware of boring yourself.

After working with one of these ski tips for a while, it might be a good idea to try a relaxing or centering exercise suggested in Chapter 5 (What to Do About It) or to take a "shouldless" run or two.

A "shouldless" run is one in which you ski ignorant. Erase all "shoulds" from your mind. Or an "anarchy" run. A run in which you say Fie! to everything you have been told. Do exactly what you feel like doing. Turn on your inside ski. Sit back. Throw your hip out. Ski like a man. Feel free.

Take Denise McCluggage's good advice. The important thing, Denise pointed out in a conversation with Elissa, is for us not to get "stuck," not to get stuck in the specific or in the general, not to get stuck in the technical or the attitudinal. Don't get stuck keeping your knees apart or keeping your act together. The flexibility to move from feeling to doing, from attack to retreat is what we're aiming for.

9

Equipment:
The Tools of the Game

Skis, boots, poles, and bindings are the tools we need to make the turns and do the maneuvers we want to do. Unless you are enthralled, as many skiers are, by design specifications and test-lab data, it is not necessary to understand ski equipment so well that you can manufacture a pair of skis in your basement. It is very helpful, however, to understand how the characteristics of ski equipment affect your skiing.

The way we turn and move on skis and the kind of equipment we use are inseparable. As ski technology developed (release bindings and fiberglass replacing long thongs and wood), ski technique changed. As ski technique changed (graduated-length teaching methods and freestyle were introduced, for instance), equipment was modified to meet the needs. The more you know about both the way you ski and the characteristics of ski equipment, the less likely you are to make mistakes in buying the skis, boots, and bindings you need.

When women set out to buy ski equipment, the first obstacle they have to overcome is the fact that they are

145

women. If women were ever relegated to the second sex, it is in the design of ski equipment. Equipment specialists, when challenged on the subject of women's equipment, tend to look maligned. Women are well taken care of, they point out. There is plenty of choice among models of skis and boots designed for lighter, smaller men.

But women are not just smaller editions of men, just as children are not just smaller editions of adults. Women are proportioned differently, jointed differently; strength relative to body mass is different. A woman can't walk into a men's store and buy a small-size man's shirt (although men's shirts are better made and cost less) and expect it to fit properly. Men with a 14-inch neck are simply not proportioned the same as a woman with a 14-inch neck. A woman can't buy a small man's ski boot and expect maximum function and ideal fit.

Women also suffer from the general assumption that they don't know what they are talking about when it comes to purchasing ski equipment. They are expected to defer to the judgment of the men around them—the ski shop salesman, friends, or relatives. Unfortunately, a great many women are willing to do that. They won't make the effort to educate themselves and won't make the protest that's necessary when what they want is not available.

This condescending attitude was typified when a Woman's Way student walked into an area ski shop to buy a new pair of boots. Helen is a good skier, trim and in condition, a part-time instructor at her home area. She is also gentle, well-mannered, and over forty. When she asked the salesman to show her a pair of high performance ski boots, he looked her over and said flatly that those boots were not for her. He recommended a much less demanding boot, knowing nothing more about her than that she was a middle-aged woman. Helen had, by coincidence, just come away from a lunchtime discussion of women's equipment needs and the attitudes that prevailed in the ski industry. She knew what she wanted, and although she was irritated, her assertiveness level was high. She refused to be intimidated, and ultimately walked out of the shop with the boots she had asked for.

Most, if not all of us, have let ourselves be intimidated into buying or renting or getting adjustments made on our equipment that were not appropriate, simply because a man made incorrect assumptions about us and the way we ski.

Women skiers as a group need to protest both to ski shops and to manufacturers. Ski equipment is a critical aspect of skiing. The right equipment enhances the skiing experience significantly and makes it easier to learn. You may not even realize how much difference it will make until at last you put together the right combination of skis, boots, and bindings for you. Whatever kinds of turns you are making, you will make them better and enjoy them more.

Women make up about 40 percent of the skiers in this country, more than 4 million females who have skied. Even half of those women potentially in the market for skis and boots and bindings selling upward of $200 (usually a lot upward) is impressive arithmetic. That combination of numbers times dollars should make someone's economic antennae quiver, should make any equipment manufacturer stand still and listen to what women have to say. Unfortunately, we've been awfully quiet, willing to let men make our choices for us. There's no good reason for that. Women developed enough clout in the auto market to push manufacturers into modifying cars. Women in skiing can do the same.

But we can't do it unless we know what we want and what is possible with ski equipment. Let's start with boots, the area where women suffer the most because their options are most limited.

Boots

The function of boots as they are designed now with a stiff shaft and firm grip on the foot is to transmit the message to the skis. If you want to put your skis on edge and you move your knee into the hill to do this, your ski will quickly follow thanks to the stiff boot which holds your ankle and foot relatively in one piece. If you were not wearing stiff boots, the movement of the knee would be partially absorbed by the ankle and foot.

The stiff high shaft also helps you deliver pressure on the skis where you want it to be—forward, back, center—without losing your balance. You can push the shaft forward because ski boots are hinged, either literally hinged with a mechanical device or by a softened shaft in the area of the ankle.

The better a skier you are, the stiffer the boot you will want, because your message will be transmitted faster to the skis. Beginners and intermediates will be happier with boots that are less stiff. Beginners and intermediates make a lot of mistakes in skiing—in the timing, edging, and radius of their turns, in their reactions to irregularities in terrain. They may react to a series of ruts, for instance, by edging or releasing the edge or by putting pressure forward or backward when it is inappropriate to do so. A high-performance boot will transmit the message immediately and the skis will react quickly. The beginner will end up in a tangle. A softer boot will "forgive" those errors by taking more time to transmit the message. While the command to edge is on the way to the skis, the beginner or intermediate may have thought better of it. She still has time to modify the maneuver.

If boots are too stiff, an intermediate woman usually lacks the strength to push forward and transmit the pressure to the front of the skis when it's necessary as well as to stay in balance on her skis. She can't absorb the shock of irregular terrain because moving back and forth on the skis requires too much effort to push the boot. As a result, she's jolted and thrown off balance. A softer boot permits a proper amount of flexibility.

Here's what to look for besides light weight and simple design when buying a ski boot.

Materials. The outer shell of ski boots today is made of synthetic materials, some of which are better than others. The best are made of polyurethanes, polyethylenes, and nylons which can combine strength, stability, and light weight, and are adaptable to heat and cold (as when going in and out of a ski lodge).

The inner shell of a ski boot is usually formed from a resilient and insulating material that cushions the foot and protects it from the hard outer shell. Some models have the ability to mold to the foot.

Buckles. Boots have from one to five buckles; the rule of thumb used to be the more buckles the more support. Formerly, two- and three-buckle boots were designed only for women and children and once-a-year skiers who theoretically did not need stiffness and support. However, new designs have been reengineered so that some high-performance models now have only two or three buckles. Most have four to five buckles. Buckles should be relatively easy to fasten and have some adjustment capability. Boots stretch, feet change from day to day and from the beginning of the season to the end, and buckles should allow for this.

Forward lean. Most boots these days are built with a certain amount of forward lean. That is, the shaft tilts forward when the boot is sitting still on the floor, empty of a foot. Racers look for more forward lean. Recreational skiers need less. Too much forward lean puts great strain on the thigh muscles, and simply holding the body up is exhausting.

If you're an intermediate skier, ask for an intermediate boot. If it's designed by a reputable manufacturer, it should have approximately the right degree of forward lean. That is, it should have more forward lean than a beginner's boot but less than an expert's.

Warmth. The boots should keep your feet warm when wearing only one pair of socks. They should also keep your feet dry. That's hard to tell in the ski shop, but you have to trust the manufacturer and the ski shop in some things.

Padding. Beginners and intermediates especially should look for sufficient padding at the collar (the top of the shaft) and in the tongue. Shins and the front of the ankle can take a real beating when you're just beginning to ski and learning to ski harder. As you become more expert and ski more often, the tissue gets tougher (or else you get used to the pain).

How to get a fit. Fit is crucial in a ski boot. No matter how expensive the boot, if it does not fit properly, it will not function properly and your feet and lower legs will probably be in pain.

Do not expect your ski-boot size to be the same as your shoe size. Depending on the shape of your foot—length of toe, height of instep, amount of fleshiness—your foot may fit into a boot as much as two sizes smaller than your street shoe. More typically, a ski boot will be one to one and a half sizes smaller.

Try on a pair of boots. The big toe should be just shy of the front of the boot when you're standing. As you walk and bend forward (and ski), the foot will move back in the boot a little.

The toes and the ball of the foot will spread when they're loaded with weight, as when you get far forward on your skis. There should be enough room in the boot to accommodate this spread, but not so much room that the foot can move around inside the boot. If your foot slops in the boot, you can lose control of your skis and the rubbing will eventually irritate your foot.

Most boots these days come with an arch built in. It may be too high for some and not high enough for others. If you have arch problems with shoes you will probably have similar problems with ski boots. However, arches can be built up or cut down inside the boot.

Women often literally get the shaft in a ski boot. A woman's calf flares out lower down on the leg than a man's calf. A shaft designed for a man's leg will frequently catch a woman right in the bulge of the calf. Even boots designed for beginner and intermediate women rarely have a scaled-down shaft, although the collar may be flared and somewhat more padded than a man's boot.

The top of the shaft should hit slightly below where the calf muscle begins to bulge. If it rises higher than that, it's going to hurt and cut off circulation; too low, control is forfeited.

To get the right fit in a boot, it's not enough to try them on. Stand up and take a few steps as you do in a shoe store. Plan on walking around the shop for at least ten to fifteen minutes. Walk, jump, stand, bend forward, bend down, imitate your ski movements as best you can.

After you have had the boots on a while, flex your ankles as if you were skiing. The heel should not lift up much. However, it shouldn't be tight either. It is not constriction but the design of the boot that should keep your heel snug. Women with narrow heels may use a heel wedge to lift the heel slightly into a snug position. You should also be able to detect the beginning of pressure points (usually around the ball of the foot or over the instep), and a too high or too stiff shaft.

Having outlined what to look for to find a good ski boot, you should know that you're not going to have an easy time finding it, particularly if you are an advanced skier.

Ski-boot manufacturers are either operating on the

theory that women never get to be expert skiers or by the time they do, their whole physiology has changed and they're just like men anyway.

Beginner and intermediate boots are made in women's models. The boot is molded on a woman's last to accommodate her differently proportioned foot, and it may be somewhat less stiff than the man's beginner or intermediate boot.

But when women are ready for a stiffer, advanced boot, they must buy men's boots. Few boot manufacturers make men's boots small enough to fit many women's feet. Usually a size 5 is the smallest man's boot made. And even if you can find a size 5, the heel will probably be too wide and it will probably be a miniature version of a size 10 or 11. That means a size 6 boot has the same buckles as a size 10, but the buckles are necessarily closer together, clasp the foot in different places, and are difficult to buckle. And the shaft is probably too high and *too* stiff, too difficult to flex forward because of the relative differences in strength between a size 5 woman and a size 5 man (or a size 7 or 8, for that matter).

A few boot manufacturers do have their antennae up and are now beginning to make high-performance women's boots. At least one manufacturer is introducing a complete line of women's boots which includes models for advanced and expert women. One or two other manufacturers are making what they call "unisex" boots (if that's possible). These boots do come in a large range of sizes and widths and although they are designed primarily for men, they seem to fit many women comfortably.

Meanwhile, as the ski industry is working on recognizing women, ski boots that don't fit perfectly can be modified quite a bit. You can add heel lifts, rework the arch, move or add bits and pieces to the inner shell to relieve pressure or add support, even shave off parts of the outer shell on the inside to ease the flex or get the fit you need. Don't do that hastily. Best to ski in the boots a bit and then have them modified.

You can also use cants or work with orthotics to change the angle of your leg to the ski's surface. Most people's legs tilt in or out; if the tilt is pronounced it can affect edge control. You'll have some indication of whether you have a problem by the way your street shoes show wear—always worn down first on the outside of the heel, for example.

Cants—thin wedges—placed under one side of the foot or the other will square the foot and the ski to the snow. Some boots have a slight cant built in already. Some boots allow wedges to be added inside the inner sole. You can measure the degree of cant needed on a machine which most ski shops have available. Some skiers with more pronounced foot problems are finding orthotic devices— molds fitted to the foot and worn inside the boot to reposition and stabilize the foot—helpful.

Women who are extremely knock-kneed may want to investigate cants and orthotic correction. One or the other sometimes does the trick.

Skis

Skis are made of various natural and synthetic materials. With these materials, a number of different characteristics are built into the ski. These are the characteristics discussed in ski magazines and manufacturers' brochures in language that usually makes us want to flip the pages quickly. Stick with us and you too can drop terms like "torsional rigidity" into your lift-line chitchat.

Swing weight. The heavier the swing weight, the heavier the ski is in the midsection relative to tip and tail and the more easily the ski will pivot.

Side cut. Skis are narrower in the middle than at front and back. This "waist" is called the side cut. A deep side cut (a narrow waist) is better for short, quick turns; a shallow side cut (wider waist) is better for long, easy turns.

Flex. The ski's stiffness or resistance to bending. Because of her lighter weight and relatively lesser strength, a woman will usually want a softer flex than a man.

Camber. If you put the ski flat on the floor, there will be an arch in the middle of the ski, like the arch of your foot. This is called camber and it helps distribute your weight along the length of the ski. To check the amount of camber in a pair of skis, put them base to base and note the space between them in the middle of the ski.

Torsional rigidity. A characteristic that keeps the skis operating as one unit—the tips and tails don't flop around—but allows some flexibility to absorb shocks. Better skiers, particularly skiers who make carved turns, look for more torsional rigidity; racers look for the most. Like auto racers, ski racers require a stiffer suspension than do Sunday drivers or Sunday skiers.

Width. The narrower a ski is, the more quickly it will move from edge to edge, the more responsive and more precise your turns can be. The wider the ski, the more forgiving it is; it gives you time to change your mind before you change your edges.

Length. The longer the ski, the more stable it is at speed. A longer ski is less sensitive to shocks from irregularities in terrain and has more of a tendency to stay in its assigned "track." Shorter skis are easier to turn. Skis range from 120 centimeters (very short, only for the first day of learning via the graduated-length method) to over 200 centimeters, usually preferred only by expert skiers or very tall skiers.

Skis do not come wrapped in pink for girls and blue for boys to make it easy for us. There are beginner's, intermediate's and expert's skis; there are stiffer and softer skis, there are longer or shorter skis. There is a confusion of choices.

How should you select a ski?

Beginners should look for a wider, stiffer, shorter ski. Beginners do not carve turns, but steer and skid them; wider, stiffer skis are easier to skid.

Intermediate skiers, just beginning to carve their turns but still skidding a lot, can look for a narrower, softer ski, still on the short side. Softer skis are easier to push into reverse camber at the times when you do carve your turns, but the shorter ski generates less friction when you slide your turns. You can make both kinds of turns more easily.

Advanced skiers should look for a somewhat stiffer, high-performance ski in longer lengths and a narrower side cut, which will allow it to carve more smoothly. They are harder to push into reverse camber, but once they are pushed into that arc, the "advanced" skis will hold at speed and on the steep, and will stay in their assigned track. They are also more responsive to your commands.

Relative to their height, women usually weigh less and are less strong than a man. They should seek a somewhat softer flex in whatever model ski they choose in order to be able to push it into reverse camber, push it into an arc. That does not mean a ski like pudding, however; it means a slightly less stiff ski.

So-called "recreational" model skis are designed for the less strong, less advanced skier and are easier to learn on. However, we recommend getting onto a competition or high-performance ski as quickly as possible because those are the skis which will do what we're aiming for—a precise carved turn. If you choose a ski graded a little beyond your ability, it will push you a little in your learning.

Among those high-performance skis, you'll find slalom and giant slalom models. The slalom skis are designed for quick, precise turns and harder snow. Giant slalom skis are for faster speeds and long-radius turns on more open terrain. These models have quite a bit of versatility, so don't feel you need two pairs of skis if you ski mostly in the eastern hard pack and take an occasional vacation in the western powder.

Again, advanced women skiers will spend a lot of time shopping. High-performance skis are designed for men and they are often too stiff, unless you are a serious racer or ski very fast. To find a ski soft enough, an expert woman may have to compromise on side cut or width or compromise on her turn. Rather than be compromised, we should make noise to manufacturers about offering softer-flex models in expert skis.

What length ski do you need? The proper length is related to height, weight, and ability. The taller, heavier, and more expert a skier you are, the longer the ski you will need. If you are tall and heavy and not so expert, subtract some centimeters. If you are small, light, and a bomb on skis, add a few centimeters. Ski manufacturers and magazines publish charts from time to time which give guidelines on relating ski length to height, weight, and ability.

You can experiment with length by renting or trying demonstration skis.

If you're a beginner we recommend that you spend a season or more—depending on how well and how often you ski—renting. The quality of rental equipment has improved considerably with advanced technology. If you think your ability will increase quickly, you will not want to invest in skis, boots, and bindings that must be upgraded next season. Ski shops and rental shops now rent high-performance skis as well as beginner and intermediate models.

When you're ready to buy, take advantage of demonstration programs at ski areas. Some women feel shy about trying out skis as if they were unworthy to get something for nothing or don't know enough about skis to tell the difference anyway. You are getting something for nothing when you try demos. You are getting an education about skis so you can tell the difference in what flex, what lengths are best for you. Ask questions and don't be afraid of sounding dumb. Ask if the skis you are trying are stiff or soft, if they're intended for ice or powder. Tell the demo people what kind of skier you are and ask for advice. If you don't like the model they recommend, say so and ask for another. That's what they're there for. They're gambling that you will like a pair of their skis well enough to buy them—a not inconsiderable investment.

Bindings

Ski bindings are designed to hold the boot to the ski and at the same time let go of the boot under stress, as when your ski is going in one direction and your leg in another. If the binding doesn't release, something has to give. That is how legs get broken, ligaments torn, tendons ruptured.

Bindings come in one-piece and two-piece styles. The two-piece type consists of a heel piece and a toe piece. Your boot is held at the heel and toe while the boot sole rests on the ski. Under stress, either toe or heel or both can release.

The second type is a plate binding. The boot is held on a single plate which attaches to the ski, and the whole plate releases under stress.

The plate binding is considered safer by insurance companies because there is less room for human error. Release is not affected by a warped or worn boot, for instance. Therefore, most rental shops use them. Some types of plate bindings are very difficult to put back on if they release in a fall. And some skiers do not like them because the plate puts another layer of material between ski and boot, making the foot that much less sensitive to what's happening under the ski and requiring that you move your foot more to put your ski on edge.

If you prefer a heel and toe combination, it is very important that the bindings you choose are compatible with your boots. Not all bindings work with all boots, although various international standards committees are trying to change that. Buy the boots first, because they are harder to fit, and then choose from among bindings that will accommodate that boot.

Incidentally, it is not wise to mix heel and toe from different manufacturers. Sometimes it works, but it's a risk and one which only a bindings expert can advise you on. So don't take a heel from Cousin Maude and a toe piece from the discount rack and pat yourself on the back for getting a bargain. The doctor bills will eat up what you saved and then some.

A binding should be able to release under more pressure or less pressure as your ability, strength, and the type of snow you ski in changes. It should not release too quickly, however. You want a binding that offers "anti-shock" capability, a binding that can, in effect, change its mind about releasing. If, for instance, you're coming down hard off a mogul and your foot and ski twist slightly, the binding will sense that as a signal to release. However, you recover quickly and take the weight off that ski. If the binding continues on its way and releases, you'll be in a lot more trouble than if you had simply fallen. You want the binding to sense quickly that the pressure is off and return to center. Most good bindings will do that.

Small, light women may have to shop a bit to find a suitable binding. There are so-called light-spring bindings often recommended for women and some men skiers. If the woman is a strong expert skier, however, the light spring may not be suitable.

Spend money on bindings. Brown-bag lunch, skip movies, scrimp where you must to invest in quality. Generally speaking, the better the quality of binding, the safer it is and the more range of adjustment it has. If you are light in weight, the tension can be set low.

Always have the bindings installed and set by a reputable ski shop. Always have them mounted using the boots you will be skiing in. If you get new boots, even the same model, recheck the bindings. When you go to pick up the skis and newly mounted bindings, take your boots with you and have the shop check the release right there.

Also check for play in the foot between the boot and a toe-heel binding. There should be just about enough room to slip in a credit card between the bottom of the boot and the antifriction device. If there is more than that, or if there is any rattling up and down or any side-to-side play, you will lose accuracy in edging.

Always have an antifriction device mounted between the sole of the boot and the ski, just under the front of the boot. This is where the most weight is centered and where friction would be greatest when release is necessary. An antifriction device (AFD, slide plate, slip plate) is a thin piece of slippery synthetic material (Teflon, other nonstick synthetics) which is screwed right onto the ski. Many bindings now are sold with ski brakes which have an AFD built in. Ski brakes keep the ski from racing down the mountain when it comes off, just as a safety strap does. But a safety strap keeps the ski attached to you where it can "windmill" and cause injuries.

Poles

PSIA technical director Horst Abraham once wrote that ski poles act as "whiskers" in the snow, just like a cat's whiskers. They give you feedback about the state of your balance and/or imbalance, and to some extent about the variations in the terrain you're crossing. They're also useful to set and hold rhythm, to help stabilize your body position, to help with unweighting, and to help you turn.

Design of poles is not related to skill, so buy the best you can afford immediately. Don't ask for a beginner's pole.

Look for light weight, strength, and swing weight. A light swing weight means the poles are easy to swing forward; they will be more sensitive to the snow and less fatiguing to maneuver. Baskets are fairly standard in size, although they may differ in shape.

Poles come with a loop grip or with a so-called saber grip, the latter like the handle of a saber where a part of the grip circles the back of your hand to stabilize it. The loop grip comes with a loop of leather or a synthetic which loops around the hand and wrist. The saber grip was developed because some felt that certain types of ski injuries, such as sprained thumbs and dislocated shoulders, were related to the loop grip. It is certainly more convenient for getting on and off lifts. However, some experts believe that the loops allow more freedom of movement with the pole than does the saber grip. Also, if you drop a pole with a saber grip you've dropped it; it's not there dangling from your wrist. Choose whichever you're more comfortable with.

Measure the proper size of pole in the shop by turning the pole upside down, putting the handle on the floor, and grasping it beneath the basket. If your arm is horizontal to the floor or slightly less, the pole is about the right length for you.

Taking Care of Your Equipment

We thought at first of putting this section into an appendix. We decided not to do so because the proper maintenance of skis is crucial to their proper performance. No matter how good a pair of skis you are on, they will not do what you want them to or what they should do if they are not taken care of.

A lot of women abdicate the responsibility of taking care of their own skis because it is, they tell themselves too technical, too complicated. They've never been mechanically apt, no one ever showed them how. Negative on all of the above except the last. And we're about to tell you how.

Tuning Skis

Skis require the most maintenance. Edges must be kept sharp and clear—no nicks or burrs, no rust, running surfaces flat and slippery. Theoretically skis should come from the factory with an absolutely flat running surface. They rarely do. They are sometimes concave—they "cave" up from the edges, making a slight arch. Or they are convex, bulging down from the edges. Skis also develop concave or convex bases from being skied on. You don't want either of those conditions. A concave ski base will track—slide straight—but it won't turn. A convex base will turn easily, but the skis won't edge well.

You can tell whether the running surface is concave or convex by holding a straight edge (metal ruler, cabinet scraper) across the base. Prop the tail of the ski on your shoulder or on a table or chair. Hold the ski up to the light so that light shines down along the running surface of the ski against the straight edge. If light shines through under the ends of the rule at the sides of the ski as you move the straight edge up and down the running surface, then the ski base is convex. If it shines through under the center of the ruler (except in the groove in the center of the ski which is supposed to be there) then it is concave. If it is concave, as is most often the case coming from the factory, then it is necessary to file down the edges until you have a flat surface.

You can do this yourself with a file but it takes a long time and is a tricky procedure. Leveling the base of a ski is best done by a reliable ski shop where they have the proper tools to do it quickly and the experience to do it right. Make it part of your beginning of the season tune-up on your skis. Ask the shop to level the bases, sharpen the edges, adjust and check the bindings, and hot-wax the skis to seal the running surfaces and make them glide. You can check on the shop, however, either by the straight-edge method just described or quickly by rubbing the ski tips together when the tails of the skis are on the ground, bases together. When skis are concave near the tip, there's a clacking sound because only the edges are making contact. If they've just been waxed this does not work. You must wait until the wax wears off.

Edges should have a sharp, 90° angle, be rounded or dulled at the tip, with no nicks or burrs (tiny irregularities, usually caused when you've skied over a rock or over someone's brand new $400 Rocket Specials). The tips are dulled to keep the ski from "hooking." If the edges of the tips are sharp, they may grab as you're making a turn and they'll keep on pulling you around the turn against your will.

For the rest of the season, you can keep your own edges sharp.

You will need:
—an 8-, 10-, or 12-inch mill bastard file
—a file card (to clean the file of scrapings)
—emery paper or fine sandpaper
—a small sharpening stone or whetstone, such as knives are sharpened with

All these are available cheaply from your friendly neighborhood hardware store, or, more conveniently, in a complete kit at ski shops.

After every skiing day, check the edges by eye and with your hand (be careful of slivers in your hand) for burrs and nicks—tiny dents or rough spots in the metal. Use the whetstone to smooth the burrs. First run the stone along the running surface of the edge, and then along the side at a right angle.

Periodically, depending on how often you ski, and on the snow conditions, you should file the edges.

Turn the skis base up. Ideally, you should fasten them to a work table with a pair of vises. But after you become experienced you can prop them in a corner, tip tucked into the angle of the wall, tail braced with your foot. What you want is that the ski be held steady so that it doesn't slip as you're pulling the file. Take the file and lay it across the base of the ski at the top, the handle of the file to the left. The file should be at about a 45° angle with the ski; it should not form a cross with the ski but have one end (in this case the handle end) tilted slightly up. Put pressure over the ski edges with your thumbs and pull down slowly and firmly. Keep the pressure on the left and right even, just over the edges. Use as few strokes as possible—two or three to go the length of the ski. Go over the ski a couple of times. It is not necessary to push down hard, but it is necessary to keep the file flat. If you bow it by holding it too far from the edge of the ski, you will end up with sloping edges.

Clean the file with a file card. Now turn the ski on its side—a vise is more important here, but brace it between your legs if you have to—and file the edge. Again, make sure the file is flat against the edges. If it tilts to the right or left, you won't have a 90° angle, but an edge that skews off on a slant. Edge files that have a 90° angle built in are available for the inexperienced or insecure. Keep the pressure firm and even; pull down, using as few strokes as possible, to the tail. Do the same to the other side of the ski.

Now run the top of your thumbnail lightly down the edge. If it's sharp enough, it will shave a little sliver of nail.

Use the emery paper to dull the tip to about the level of the start of the groove in the base of the ski, and dull the last inch or so of the tail. Run the emery paper *lightly* over the entire edge to take off any filing burrs or shavings still clinging.

If you've never done this before, it's helpful to watch someone else do it before you try. Your ski shop might let you watch. If the area you ski has a race program, slip into the race hut and watch the racers tune up their skis; or into the ski school early in the morning. Or ask a friend who does her own skis.

You can also wax your own skis with an ordinary household iron. Put your ski, base up, on a flat (protected) surface. Plug in the iron and set it to a medium heat. Hold the block of wax against the iron and let it melt and dribble onto the ski on either side of the groove. If the wax starts to smoke, then your iron is too hot. Now iron the wax onto the ski, smoothing and spreading it over the base with the iron, just as you would iron a skirt or a tablecloth. Don't linger too long in one place. If wax has dribbled into the groove, clean it out with a coin. Don't use too much wax. Now scrape the base with your cabinet scraper to smooth uneven or excess wax. Your skis are ready.

Maintaining Boots and Bindings

Read the instruction material that comes with your bindings. It will tell you what special care your particular bindings need. Make sure your bindings are sprayed with silicone at least at the beginning of each season. It keeps the moving parts moving. Also make sure they are clean, free of dust, mud, dirt, on all the visible surfaces. Check particularly for mud and debris if you're skiing in the spring or any time when the snow is thin or mushy and the dirt surfaces through the snow. Spray with silicone.

You should also check the release every day you ski. If you don't, at least have it checked at the start of and occasionally during the season. It's some insurance that they're functioning the way they should.

Boots need to be kept clean—particularly the soles—and dry inside. If the inner shell comes out easily, take it out at the end of the day to let it dry more thoroughly when it's wet from perspiration and snow. Or use a blow drier. Broken buckles can usually be repaired at a ski shop.

Understanding ski equipment, keeping it in working order, doesn't take a lot of time nor does it take an engineering degree, as some women and men tend to think. What we need to know is what characteristics of a ski, boot, or binding will best suit the kind of skier we are and the kind of body we have. Do read the ski magazines and manufacturers' brochures and any books you have that you think might be helpful. But read them with a critical eye—manufacturers are, of course, touting their own products; ski magazines feed you reams of facts, including tables of measurements, from length to swing weight to torsional rigidity. They will tell you what the measurements mean and what the outer parameters should be, but they won't tell you which is the best buy. Advertisers might be offended. You'll have to read between the lines or study the measurements carefully to form your own opinion about whether the ski or boot will do what it should do and how the qualities of the ski suit you.

If you've put some effort into analyzing the kind of equipment you want, tried demos or a variety of rentals, and made a decision about what you want, don't be afraid to ask for it. Ski-shop people frequently get annoyed when a customer asks for something on the basis of what they've read in a book or magazine. Don't let their annoyance psych you out. It's your money. More important, it's the equipment you'll be skiing on. If someone dictates your choice of equipment, you won't be able to make it your own.

Part of the pleasure of skiing is in making friends with your equipment, in learning to trust your skis, your bindings, feel comfortable in your boots. If you and your equipment are constantly at war with each other, either because someone else picked it out for you or you don't understand what the ski can actually do or not do, then you will be drained and exhausted at the end of the day, just as if you had spent the day fighting with a colleague.

Once you and your skis make friends, once you make a commitment to trust and take care of your equipment, it is truly as if a great burden has been lifted. You know that the skis will do what you want them to, that your bindings will protect you, that your boots will support you, and you can concentrate on skiing and learning and having fun.

10

Taking Care of Yourself on a Mountain

A certain mystique has evolved around skiing. It reflects the skiers' image of themselves as Very Special People—people who have overcome cold, inconvenience, expense, and the acquisition of complicated skills and can now stand confidently at the top of a mountain ready to speed down in a series of picturesque turns.

As with any elite group, certain rituals evolve that serve to identify the membership. The way you carry your equipment from car to base lodge, the way you behave in a lift line, etiquette on a ski slope, conversations on a chair lift and in a bar after skiing serve to identify a skier. Some of the rituals are codified in "The Skiers' Courtesy Code"; some are merely understood. Certainly, skiers are set apart by the clothes they wear. Like many rituals, however, dressing for skiing has a practical basis. In this case, it is self-preservation.

Ski clothes are part of the fun of the sport. Buying fashionable clothes in flattering colors may make you feel good about yourself. If you feel good about the way you look, you may feel better about the way you ski. The primary purpose of ski clothes is not to keep you psychologically high, however; it is to keep you warm and dry.

Women Get Colder

Women complain more of the cold than men do. This may be because women get colder than men. This probably has a biological basis but the causes are fuzzy for now. One theory suggests that it has to do with a process called vascularization which relates to the amount of blood pumped to the surface of the skin. Because women seem to have less capacity to carry oxygen in their blood, and because apparently their hearts are smaller than men's (even relative to size and body weight), they may not get as much warming blood to the outer surface and extremities as men. Or hormonal differences may account for variation in the way the sexes sense and control body temperature. So don't hesitate to add the extra layer of clothing even if the male skiers in your group say you don't need it. You're the best judge of that.

The most effective way to keep warm is to dress in layers. The colder it is, the more layers you add: underwear, turtleneck, sweater, ski pants, parka. Layers keep you warm because air is trapped between them and serves as insulation, in the same way a porous fiberglass traps air and serves as insulation for a house.

Most of us can put together those layers of clothing from various items around the house, but when you're pulling out the sweaters and T-shirts to build a ski outfit, look for two things: clothes that are tight at the wrist and neck and at the waist or hip, and at the ankle. This holds the warm air in. Turtlenecks are popular with skiers, because they seal the warm air in effectively.

The outer layer of clothing should also be water resistant. Some skiers like to ski in jeans, but jeans get wet from flying snow, falling snow, or falls in the snow. Wet fabric is cold; it draws the body heat out and can chill you faster than you think possible. A water-resistant parka and overpants are good priorities in a clothing budget.

Long underwear should be light, comfortable next to the skin, and it should absorb perspiration. People do perspire when they ski and if it isn't absorbed away from the body, the skin becomes clammy and uncomfortable. Cotton, silk, and very fine wool will do that (coarser wool is itchy), as will some combinations of cotton and synthetics or wool and synthetics. There are also some miracle fibers that insulate and absorb and have the advantage of being able to be rinsed out and dried overnight.

Some women find their ankles irritated occasionally, even blistered, by seams in long underwear. Look for a flat seam which will minimize the irritation. Some women like to wear leotards, either with or without feet, instead of long underwear when the weather isn't too cold, because they cut down on bulk. Nylon leotards or panty hose are not absorbent, however, and if they have feet, your foot may slip inside the boot causing you to give up some control. Leotards cannot replace long johns on a cold day. Some women reject long underwear or bulky sweaters in the interest of a streamlined silhouette. Icicles are streamlined too, but you wouldn't want to be one.

When you're buying outerwear, parka and pants or jacket and overalls, look for a tightly woven, water-resistant fabric with locked seams so water won't seep in. Also look for zippers that work. (A spray of silicone or a bar of soap rubbed along the zipper will help when it gets sticky.) Most jackets and many overalls or pants are designed with a layer of insulation between shell (the outer layer) and lining. The insulation can be anything from down to pieces of kapok. Stay away from kapok but don't necessarily go for down simply because it's the most expensive. The technology of synthetic insulation (fill, it's called) is such that it can be as warm or warmer than down, is extremely lightweight, resilient (bounces back after being compressed in a suitcase, for instance), and retains some insulating properties even if it gets wet.

Ski with a hat if it's cold. A great deal of body heat is lost through the head. Your head may not feel cold, but that's probably because the body's first priority is pumping blood to the brain; while it's doing that to your bare head, the rest of you will get chilled. Wearing a hat can make an amazing difference in how warm you feel. If you get too warm, take off the hat.

Feet are usually well protected by ski boots and one pair of wool or thermal socks. Should they get chilled while you're standing in the lift line, for instance, often they will warm up quickly when you begin to ski, as legs pump up and down and feet move, demanding more blood for those parts. There is no doubt, though, that some ski boots are warmer than others.

Hands, gripped around poles, move relatively little. Mittens help contain warmth more than gloves; light gloves (cotton, soft wool) inside mittens are warmest of all. Gloves inside gloves may also work but gloves constrict more than mittens, so make sure the outer gloves are big enough. Some skiers find there is a definite loss of "feel" when they wear mittens and use them only when the weather is bitter.

Eat Hearty

Women may also get colder than men because they don't eat enough. Conscious of weight, many women skip breakfast or nibble on grapefruit and lettuce leaves. A ski holiday is not the time to diet. Carbohydrates in particular, anathema to dieters, are quickly converted to energy; a good breakfast—oatmeal with raisins, eggs and bacon *and* bran muffins—will help keep you warmer.

Avoid heavy meals in the middle of your skiing day when it's cold. Heavy food or lots of food in the stomach sends the blood supply rushing to the digestive system to assist in digestion. When it's in the stomach, it's not at the periphery of your body to do its warming work. Stay with carbohydrates, but don't sit down to a three-course meal at lunch.

Oranges are favored skier snacks not only because the natural sugar provides energy, but because there's lots of liquid in them to stave off dehydration. Actually, dehydration is not a particular danger for most Alpine skiers; they usually don't throw off that much perspiration. If it's spring and you're still skiing in your winter parka, however, you should be aware of replenishing body fluids.

Drinking coffee, tea, alcohol makes you colder although it may for the moment give you a warm glow. So does smoking. So does tension. Your blood vessels will soon constrict and make it more difficult for the blood and fluids that help keep you warm to get to the extremities.

Why all the emphasis on keeping warm? Aside from the fact that being cold is unpleasant and may make you more susceptible to disease, it also makes you more susceptible to injury. Cold muscles, contracted muscles, are more vulnerable to injury, because they are more brittle. Don't start a run if you're feeling chilled on the theory that skiing will warm you. If you are cold when you get off the chair lift, take a few minutes to stretch and bend, hop on your skis, do shoulder rolls and drops. This will not only warm you up but help relax you as well.

The Face Factor

Most of us have heard of wind chill, but it's more than a number on a handy little pocket chart. A gentle breeze, a little more than two miles an hour, can carry off three times as much body heat as would be lost if the air were calm. The stronger the wind, the more body heat is lost. At ski areas, winds of twenty or thirty miles an hour are not unusual, and on unprotected summits, they have been known to gust over fifty miles an hour. When winds are blowing, ski clothes should be zipped up at wrists, ankles, waist, or hip. Pulling up a turtleneck or using a bandana as a mask can protect mouth and nose; pull your hat down over your ears.

Protecting exposed skin in extreme cold helps prevent frostbite. Frostbite occurs in very cold weather when the water in the cells of the outer layer of skin becomes frozen and the cells rupture. The pieces of frozen water and tissue can block the blood flow in the capillaries, causing the skin to whiten and die. The surface skin regenerates itself very quickly, but you don't want the condition to penetrate any deeper than the surface layer. If the weather is very cold, have the friends you're skiing with check each other frequently for white spots on exposed skin. If your toes or fingers are feeling particularly numb and stiff, check them as well. If you spot frostbite, warm the area immediately with a warmer part of your body—the palm of your hand to the face, fingers under the arm (inside the parka). Don't rub. Frostbitten skin is sensitive and will abrade quickly. When you get inside, thaw fingers or toes with warm, not hot water. Hot water can cause burns.

Wind, cold, and sun on a ski slope can dehydrate the skin quickly. Creams and oily or greasy lotions do not replace the water lost from your skin; what they do is form a film on the skin that keeps water from being lost as quickly. So if you are a user of creams and lotions, put them on before you go skiing when they will do the most good. Hair also gets dry; wear a hat or use conditioners to coat the hair shaft.

Beware—we cannot stress this too strongly—of sunburn, especially when you are skiing at high altitudes, especially when you are skiing in the spring. High-altitude burns can put you in the hospital at worst; at the least they can be painful and ugly. It's not enough to wear a hat with a visor. Fifty percent of the burn you receive when you're skiing comes from sun reflecting off the snow, up onto your face.

Zinc oxide may still be the best protection against the sun, but most people simply won't use it, except on the tips of their noses, because it is sticky, clings to clothes and hands, and tends to make them look like circus clowns.

So look for a strong sunscreen lotion. Many sunscreen products now carry an SPF (sun protection factor) number as recommended by the Food and Drug Administration. The higher the number, the greater the protection against the sun. Numbers higher than 6 offer extra protection (many of them contain a chemical known as PABA which filters the ultraviolet light that does the damage). Depending on your skin's sensitivity to the sun, go for an SPF number of 6 or more when you ski at high altitude or in the spring.

Before you go out, apply it liberally on all exposed skin including ears and back of neck, if your hair is short or you wear it up. Take a small tube or bottle with you so you can renew it. What happens is that while the warm sun feels good on your body and face, it does not feel hot—the air cools your skin. Skiers unused to high altitude do not realize they're getting a burn until they look at their faces in a mirror.

Lips suffer particularly from the effects of wind, sun, and cold. If you don't wear lipstick, use lip balm or sunblock and remember to renew it often.

Use sunglasses if you're spring skiing, particularly at high altitudes. Eyes get light-sensitive because of the reflection from the snow; they may begin to tear and water. They may even feel as if they won't stay open.

Feeling Bad?

There are other effects of high altitude, including shortness of breath, headaches, loss of appetite, fatigue, slower reflexes, inability to sleep well, slight nausea, and lowered endurance. High altitude is defined for skiers as anything above 5,000 feet. The higher you go, the thinner the air and the less oxygen is delivered to your bloodstream by each breath. For most skiers it is just a nuisance. Take it easy for the first day or two—shorten the skiing day, stop often to rest, eat what appeals to you. It should take only a few days to acclimatize. However, skiers with cardiac problems or respiratory problems should check with their doctors before venturing to a high-altitude ski area.

What is the effect of menstruation on skiing? It seems to depend a lot on the individual. Studies done on racers report almost no effects generally—medals have been won at all stages of the menstrual cycle. Some skiers who are not racers, however, report various feelings of lethargy, weakness, heavy limbs, and nervousness during the days prior to menstruation. The difference between racers and ordinary skiers may have to do with physical condition and training. If you do feel lethargic, "nervous," or weak, there is no medical reason not to ski. However, you may want to slow down or stick to easier slopes for a day or so.

Should you ski when you're pregnant? Dr. Alan Guttmacher's rule of thumb is probably appropriate here—if you skied before you were pregnant, you can probably ski while you're pregnant unless you have a history of miscarriages or are still at the beginning stages of skiing where you're concerned about falling a lot. But if you're solid and stable and confident on skis you'll probably enjoy skiing while you're pregnant. We even heard of one woman who skied until she was well into her eighth month. We were more curious about where she found ski clothes to fit her than the fact that she was skiing.

What about injuries? Statistics which compare skiing to other risk sports are hard to come by, but we think that relative to the number of people who ski, the number of days they ski, and the potential for injury in the sport, skiing is by no means most dangerous. We know that the rate of injuries is getting lower all the time as ski equipment and technique improve. However, the potential for injury is there, and avoiding accidents involves common sense and respect for the environment.

Buy or rent good equipment and be absolutely sure that the bindings on your skis are set properly for your weight and ability and are in good operating condition. If you're a beginner, make sure you understand how to get in and out of the bindings. Before you step into your binding, check the bottom of your boot sole to be sure there are no lumps of snow on the bottom for these can make the binding slow to function or not function at all. Read the section on maintaining your equipment in Chapter 9.

Injury statistics indicate that women are injured more often than men, but we're no longer sure about that. In the past, injury statistics were collected by the National Ski Patrol on the basis of voluntary reports. People were either carried in or came into the patrol office to report an injury. It's believed now by some that this skewed the statistics because women were more likely than men to report minor injuries—contusions, abrasions, lacerations. Recent, more carefully controlled injury studies suggest that differences in physiology do not dictate a higher injury rate for women, that women's bones are no weaker than men's, pound for pound of body weight, and no more likely to break if bindings are set properly. What may affect injury rate is that women lack the muscle tone that men have because they are not in as good condition and do not have a history of athletic involvement.

Ski Defensively

Pay attention to your environment. Just because slopes are now groomed and packed, and rocks and stumps are removed by machines at ski areas does not mean that nature is not still in charge. Hard-pack snow can soften in less than an hour if the temperature goes up; soft snow can crust over or turn to ice almost as quickly. The slope you skied in the morning may not be the same in the afternoon. Learn to read the snow, assess it, adjust your technique to what's coming up. Watch what's happening to other skiers in front of you.

If you're whizzing down a slope that was hard pack in the morning and run into a pile of mush because rising temperatures and dozens of skiers have softened it up, it's like running into a wall. If you're not ready for it, you can go flying. Or vice versa. If you start cranking your turns with real power because yesterday afternoon the slope was mush, and discover as your skis go skating out from under you that this morning it's ice, you are in trouble. Tune in to what's happening around you, under you, ahead of you.

You don't want to hurt yourself; you don't want to hurt other skiers around you. Beginning and intermediate skiers particularly get so involved in thinking about their turns, they are completely oblivious to what's happening around them. Ski as if you were driving a car. Don't pull into an intersection of trails without checking for traffic above you. If you're skiing on a gentle slope or a runout which expert skiers are schussing, don't change lanes—begin suddenly to make wider turns or stop in a long traverse—without checking the traffic behind you. The skier behind you does have the responsibility of avoiding the skier ahead, but if you do something completely unpredictable, even the most expert skier can't stop or turn in time. If you are wearing a safety strap, a ski leash, be sure it's fastened properly.

The weather can be as unpredictable as a beginning skier, particularly when you are high-mountain skiing. If fog or a heavy snow closes in, it's easy to become disoriented and end up on the wrong trail. In a really thick fog or blizzard you can even become a victim of vertigo, because you can't tell up from down let alone which trail is which. Try to ski on trails that have definition, trails lined by trees, for instance. Don't ski in open bowls when visibility is bad. Stay on clearly marked, preferably heavily skied trails.

Most of us don't really have to be concerned with avalanches; we ski on marked and groomed trails at well-managed, safety-conscious ski areas. But some regions are more prone to avalanches than others because of heavy snowfall or the type of snow that falls. If you are excited by skiing powder or deep snow, be aware that avalanches are possible. No matter how the group of powder hounds you're skiing with might tempt you, do not go onto slopes that are not controlled for avalanches. That usually means don't ski outside the ski area boundaries no matter how beautiful and untracked the neighboring bowl is.

If you are skiing off-trail, at least be aware that avalanches are more likely to occur during and after big storms and in the spring, when the snow begins to soften.

Your Body Is Telling You Something ▬▬▬▬▬

Watch for signs of fatigue in yourself. Women may get tired more quickly than men because they are not in good condition, not because their capacity to endure is less. More subtle signs of fatigue include slower response time—you edge and turn the ski but it still keeps going straight ahead until you edge and pressure it more strongly. Your skis are getting away from you—you're sitting back and inside on your turns. You feel chilled. The slope ahead seems more difficult this time than it did last time. You're skiing more slowly without intending to. Stop for the day or at least stop for a long break.

During the first days of a new season, we may tend to try to re-create our memories of how we skied last winter. But our bodies have been taking it easy—they've been off skis for five or six months. They won't stand for it. Although enthusiasm and excitement may keep us going for the first day, rebellion will set in on the second and third days.

No matter how good you feel, you really shouldn't hop onto your skis on the first, second, or any day without warming up first. Skiing with "cold," stiff, brittle muscles will lead to tears, pulls, sprains, and pain.

Warmup exercises increase body heat which heats the muscles and makes them more flexible and responsive to nerve impulses. Breathing rate is increased gradually, getting more oxygen to the bloodstream. Fluids that lubricate the joints begin to flow more freely.

As in skiing, don't set impossible exercise goals for yourself. If you resolve to spend twenty minutes every morning before breakfast on warmups, and you only spend ten, you'll feel a failure. Don't make resolutions. Just do it.

Once you're on the hill, take advantage of the time you spend in lift lines and on the lifts by keeping muscles warmed up. In the lift line, lift your legs and walk in place; contract and relax thighs and buttocks; lift and drop your shoulders; stretch your arms to the side and to the front (without taking off someone's hat). If you begin to get chilled on a chair lift, raise and lower your thighs a few inches off the seat; swing your legs gently back and forth—very gently, so the chair doesn't sway. Move your shoulders, grip poles tightly and relax, flex your ankles bringing your tips up toward your chest (also gently).

It isn't true what some of us were taught in gym class: the more it hurts, the better we're doing.

If it hurts, don't do it, says Ben Benjamin in a book called *Sports Without Pain*. Or at least wait until you know why it's hurting. If your muscles are sore from the day before, take brief rests during the course of a long run; it gives them a chance to recover. It's a myth that working sore muscles makes them less painful. A little soreness is okay, but it should go away within a day. If it persists or doesn't moderate for a long time, check it out with a doctor or physical therapist. Take care of your body. Take a warm, not a hot bath, scrubbing with a soft brush or loofa to stimulate the skin. Add a little salt to the water if you're tense. Take a whirlpool; use a shower massage; use sauna or steam rooms if you like them.

Soreness and fatigue may be consequences of physical exertion. That doesn't mean we can't do something to minimize discomfort.

11

Putting Fear in Its Place

Women skiers are frequently pictured as timid, overcautious, fearful. But there are millions of people, men and women, who don't ski at all because they are "afraid"— afraid of breaking a leg, afraid of the cold, afraid of falling off a lift. So the woman who has committed herself to ski, even if she has only gone as far as renting equipment and signing up for her first lesson, has already modified the picture of the fearful female.

In previous chapters we have seen that the feeling that inhibits the skiing of many women is not fear, but anxiety, tension, confusion about roles, even anger and resentment. But these feelings get all tangled up with genuine fear of death or injury and are lumped together under "I'm afraid . . ."

Unlike basketball or running or tennis, skiing *is* a dangerous sport. The dangers are not only real, they can sometimes be very great. Avalanches, crevasses hidden by crusted snow, rocks, cliffs. Steep and icy slopes which send us out of control. Narrow and winding trails where trees or chair lift towers form an obstacle course if we are not on top of every turn. Blizzards, fog, bringing with them the possibility of wandering off-course. It is appropriate, even necessary, that sometimes we should feel afraid. But it is also important that we should understand that there are several faces to fear. Sometimes fear is paralyzing, sometimes it is stimulating. Sometimes it is the proper response to danger; sometimes what we label fear is the mosaic of anxiety.

The feeling or emotion which we call fear is both a psychological and a physiological state, but the physiological components can be massive. When you see danger—a cornice beginning to break, a car looming down as you cross the street, it immediately triggers a host of physiological reactions. Your heart rate increases, your blood vessels constrict, your breathing grows faster and shallower, muscles tense, your blood surges to feed the large muscles leaving the extremities cold and clammy, and your digestive system is in turmoil.

All of these reactions originate in that part of the brain called the limbic system, in both evolutionary and developmental terms one of the oldest parts of the brain. Here are the hypothalamus, pituitary gland, and a little almond-shaped nugget called the amygdala. When the amygdala is electrically stimulated in animals, even strong, aggressive predators, it arouses frenzies of fear. When our amygdalas and nearby glands are stimulated by Danger! they send messages that originated perhaps a million or more years ago. They say "fight or flight," watch out, there's a big, hungry, saber-tooth tiger in the forest ahead of you and you are the menu for dinner. The hypothalamus and pituitary glands go to work, calling for the release of adrenaline and other hormones, which in turn signal your feet to make tracks. Run or hope that the surge of chemicals released by your terrorized limbic system will make you strong enough to fight.

Fortunately, there are no saber-tooth tigers prowling the slopes of Squaw Valley or even the jungles of Manhattan. But our bodies will react in more or less the same way to what we see today as dangerous, the speeding car or the falling cornice. Souped up by the fear reaction, we will be able to leap out of the path of the car, or ski as we've never skied before to get out of the path of the surging snow. That is one way in which fear is useful.

Fear can also be a stimulant, a charging of the body's batteries to confront a situation that is dangerous but not overwhelming.

Elissa came across a child, about eight years old, standing at the top of a wicked pitch. He was hesitating, regarding the run.

"It looks pretty tough, doesn't it," Elissa said.

"It sure does," the boy answered. "It looks too tough for me, I think. Maybe I shouldn't do it."

"Well, maybe you shouldn't," Elissa said.

"But I want to," the child said emphatically.

The boy was feeling fear as he should have, but he was not in panic. He obviously thought that in spite of his fear he had the skills to ski the steep slope, the weapons to overcome the tiger.

Is It Fear or Anxiety?

Sometimes we mistake anxiety for fear. What is the difference between fear and anxiety? It is what some psychologists call the difference between the outside and the inside, the difference between reality and illusion. Whether the dangers are real or imagined, the body reacts in the same way. Anxiety starts the same physical process: tense muscles, shortened breath, accelerated heartbeat, and so forth. The symptoms of anxiety are different only in degree from the symptoms of fear. But while the symptoms of fear can sometimes be useful, the symptoms of anxiety are more likely to get in our way.

There is such a thing as a medically defined anxiety reaction, an "undefined dread or fear of an impending calamity such as death or insanity." It produces such physical symptoms as vomiting, diarrhea, urinary urgency, heart palpitations, sweating. It often, but not always, comes in the night.

Luckily, what most of us label as anxiety in ourselves is not that intense. When you rise to make your first speech to a large audience, for instance, your hands are clammy, your breath is short, your vision may even be distorted as eye muscles tense. These are signals of danger. But what is in danger is not a lost life, but a lost self-image. You are in danger of making a fool of yourself.

While your head may be able to differentiate between fear and anxiety, very often your body cannot. If you have made a wrong turn and are faced with a steep and icy slope down which expert skiers are crashing and gliding, and you have barewy achieved a passable wedge turn, then you have good and sensible reason to be afraid and your body will tell you so. Your heart will beat faster, your saliva may dry up, your breathing may become irregular and your muscles rigid. It is probably best to pay attention to what your body is telling you, to sidestep out of your predicament, to sideslip, to kick-turn, to call for help.

But often when skiers say they "fear" a slope and can't get down it, they mean they can't get down it the way they want to. They mean they may have to revert to sideslipping or a kick-turn and damage their self-image.

If you are faced with a gentle slope covered with perfect packed powder, but someone you want to impress is waiting at the bottom for you and watching you come down, your heart may beat faster, your saliva may dry up, your breathing may become irregular, and your muscles tense. Your body is telling you that there is something to fear. It doesn't know the difference at this point.

Usually, causes of anxiety are not so easy to define. If you want to ski or ski better, but believe somewhere in the back of your mind that skiing fast is an improper activity for a woman, you may feel anxious. If you think it through you are apprehensive about doing something for which you might somehow be punished, about stepping out of your "feminine" role.

Anxiety can also be a reaction to a low estimate of yourself. If you are out there doing something—skiing moguls—that you do not think you are worthy to do or capable of doing, you will feel anxious.

If you are taking a lesson and working very hard to please the instructor and the instructor does not respond as you think she should, then you become anxious.

Both fear and anxiety are distracting, you are thinking about how you feel, not about what you are doing. If you are fearful about avoiding that big clot of bodies in the middle of the slope, you are more likely to run into that clot of bodies. Like the rabbit and the snake, we are hypnotized by danger.

Anxiety also makes us shy away from problems rather than try to solve them. It exaggerates frustration so that mistakes become magnified. A fall is no longer a fall but a catastrophe.

More important in this context is that aimless anxiety impairs judgment. You may regard that mild slope as the bottom of KT22 and flee to a yet more gentle slope unanchored by the person you are trying to impress. Or you may decide that you will show everyone and simply point your skis straight down, turning neither to right nor left until your speed is so great that you can only stop by throwing yourself down or crashing into the watcher. You have done yourself a disservice in both cases, one, by underestimating your ability and fleeing imaginary danger; two, by denying the possibility of any danger.

"Intuitive" Fears

Some of our fears we seem to be born with. Fear of falling is high on the list and, as scientist Carl Sagan suggests, it's a good thing too.

If our arboreal ancestors—the tree-dwelling primates—had not been afraid of falling and protected themselves strongly against it, we wouldn't be here, at least not in our present forms. When we first begin to ski, it is possible that this primitive fear surfaces first because skiing is nothing but a series of controlled falls. As we let loose on our first straight run down a hill, as we permit ourselves not only to fall down a mountain, but even lean forward in the direction of our descent, somewhere inside us a great-great-great-great grandmother primate must be screaming, "Don't do it." We silence her quickly as we learn to control both speed and angle of descent. But as hills get steeper and longer, she will surface again from time to time. Keep in mind that she may not always be wrong before you send her back to her tree.

Women more than men seem to have a deeply rooted fear of pain and injury. This does not go back to our tree-dwelling forebears, but to our split-level dwelling mothers or grandmothers who told us, "Don't climb that tree or walk that picket fence, you'll hurt yourself." It goes back to the myth of women as porcelain dolls.

While thousands of women are now jogging, playing tennis, riding bikes, mountain climbing, to say nothing of lifting monstrous grocery bags and wiggling children, those myths of destroying our ability to bear children still attach themselves to athletics and physical activity. More particularly, they attach themselves to skiing, which is perceived as a risk sport and where the injuries that are sustained—broken ankles, broken arms—are very visible to the public eye. (TV advertisers in particular seem to revel in portraying skiers sitting in front of a cozy fire hoisting a few of the advertised brand while resting heavy leg casts on the coffee table.)

In fact, some investigators assert that women seem to have the physiological and psychological capacity to endure *more* pain than men and are not more susceptible to injury. We know that athletic women carry through pregnancy and childbirth more easily than sedentary ones. But as the authors of *Skiing from the Head Down* say, we are "wired for self-preservation," individually and tribally, and the myth that girls are weak and need to be protected persists.

Let us hope that we will not pass that message on to our girl children, and as they grow up with physical experience as part of their whole lives, not just their prepubescent years, they will not unreasonably fear pain and injury or bruises that mar their good looks.

We will put in a *caveat* for this generation. Women may sustain more injuries than men, not because they are women, but because they may have avoided athletics. Their muscles are weaker and less protective of the bones. Tendons and ligaments may be underutilized and even semiatrophied. Therefore, sprains, strains, and aches and bruises may be more prevalent among women. The solution is not to change sex or give up skiing, but to get in better shape.

While these facts may put risk of injury in its proper perspective, it is still true that there is risk involved in skiing. That is part of its appeal. While the risk of serious injury may be less than we assume, we should be aware and make a decision about whether we want to chance even that. Cathy, a Woman's Way student, reentered skiing not long ago because her six children were grown or at least of an age to fend for themselves. She had made a decision a number of years before to give up skiing because she did not want to take the risk of breaking a bone and being unable to care for her family. Of course, she subsequently took up riding a motorcycle. It would seem that risk is in the eye of the beholder.

To a great extent it is. Like Cathy, if you approach a hill with six children figuratively riding on the back of your skis, that hill is going to seem dangerous. If you are a doctor with patients depending on you, that hill is going to seem risky. To another woman, whose children are grown or whose profession is flexible enough to accommodate a plaster cast, that same slope will seem merely challenging.

The Challenge Threshold

We must all decide for ourselves what level of risk we are willing to sustain, and be sensitive to when—for us—fear that interferes replaces the anticipation of challenge.

The challenge thresholds we set for ourselves are not always, need not always be rational or consistent. We may drive our cars as if we were Janet Guthrie at Indianapolis and ski like the proverbial little old lady in tennis shoes. That's irrational, to be sure. We are far more likely to kill ourselves by driving recklessly than by skiing recklessly. But if we are fearful and anxious when we ski at speed, then it is sensible and proper to recognize that and stay within the limits we have set.

A former Olympic team racer who lives in Squaw Valley rarely skis the West Face of the mountain. She skis other slopes at Squaw equally as difficult. But she has an aversion to the West Face for some reason; skiing it makes her tense and she knows she is more apt to hurt herself. That may not be rational, but it is wise.

The challenge threshold is different for every individual. What to one woman may be titillating, to another may be terrifying. What to one is a challenge, to another is boring. The same person may have different thresholds on two different days. One day you may be cautious because you haven't had enough sleep, because you didn't eat breakfast, because you have a big exam coming up. Another day your promotion to vice-president came through and you feel as if you can take on the world. The reasons don't really matter, as it does not matter why one woman is challenged by speed and another by grace. All we need is to be aware of our own thresholds today.

We must be careful that we set our own challenges. It does not do to ski with a group of friends who are all abandon while you are feeling cautious.

"We'll do this in three turns," they shout merrily as you stand rigid at the crest of a steep slope. Maybe yesterday you did it in three turns, but if today you look down and consider yourself lucky to be able to do it in twenty-three turns, back off. Take a deep breath, do it in twenty-three turns. You're skiing for yourself, not for them. You'll catch them later and still be in one piece physically and psychologically.

If we push ourselves beyond our challenge thresholds, we are not only uncomfortable, but we are literally setting ourselves up for a fall. If we put ourselves in danger because our judgment is fogged, our muscles will be tense and unresponsive.

Whether what you are feeling is fear or anxiety, it can interfere with your skiing. The circuits in your body will be overloaded with messages of panic and you are not going to be able to receive or transmit anything else clearly. The nerve pathways you grooved with your new awareness and kinesthetic sensibility are clogged with the debris of fight or flight. You're not going to be able to turn left or right with any degree of control or grace until you clear the pathways.

On the other hand, we shouldn't set the challenge too low.

Says Stu Campbell: "Sports psychologists agree that too much fear is bad for learning but by the same token, oddly enough, they tell us that too *little* anxiety isn't good either. In fact, in any learning situation, there's an ideal level of anxiety which will produce the best performance. What they're saying is that no athlete can do well if he is scared out of his wits, of course, but if he's not 'psyched up', he is not going to do well either."

The little push we give ourselves to ski a little faster, a little harder, in more difficult conditions or on a more difficult slope than we did last week well rewards the slight nervousness—or even the considerable nervousness—we might feel before taking off. The nervousness might be a feeling of pleasure in itself.

There's a rush of anticipation, a thrill. It's an adrenal high. It's the same thrill we get on a roller coaster. It's one reason why amusement parks are proliferating in this country and why the roller coaster rides are getting more and more terrifying. We can get addicted to "adrenal burgers."

But the rewards of meeting the challenge you set for yourself are greater even than the flutter of excited anticipation.

For the woman who "fell apart" in icy and stormy conditions, to be able to ski down that steep slope with the snow blowing around her—to ski, not fast, not beautifully, but with a measure of control and assurance—would be immensely satisfying. To stand at the bottom of the slope, look up and appreciate what she had done, would bring long-term rewards: pride at having dealt with her anxiety, pleasure in her competence as a skier and as a human being, in the teamwork of body and mind which had led her to the accomplishment.

What Am I Feeling Now?

That's all easy to say, but how do you define your challenge thresholds? How do you differentiate between foolish risk and stimulating risk. How do you know if what you're feeling is fear or anxiety?

Say you're standing at the top of a long, steep, somewhat icy slope. Today you want to link your turns closer together, not make long traverses as you have done in the past. But have you made the right decision; are you setting yourself a reasonable challenge? Your heart is beating fast, your stomach is churning, and your breathing is erratic.

The first thing to do is gain control of those runaway bodily functions. Center yourself. Concentrate on your breath first and bring it back to a calm and rhythmic cycle. Now relax your tense muscles—scan your body to find out where you are most tense, breathe into those places and feel the rigidity begin to go out of them. Give yourself one of those rag doll shakes. Your heart and other involuntary functions will also begin to calm themselves.

Now look at the slope again. Don't look at the other skiers. Just look at the slope and think of it in terms of your own skill. A book called *Born to Win* offers a program for dealing with anxiety which works very effectively on the ski slopes.

1) Clarify what it is you are "afraid" of. Be very specific: "I'm afraid I'm going to fall and hurt myself; I'm afraid I'll lose control and run into another skier."

2) What is the worst that could really happen? Yes, you could fall, but would you injure your body or your ego? Could you run into another skier?

3) How would you cope if the worst happened? If you felt yourself going out of control or playing touch football with the other skiers on the hill, could you pull up and stop or slow down?

If you don't feel you could stop or regain control, then reconsider. Readjust your goals. Move to a slope that is not so steep or so crowded if you want to work on linking turns closer together. Or ski this slope using turns which you can control.

Your anxiety will diminish because you have taken the pressure off yourself. You were never in a real life-threatening situation because you had options; you did not need to ski straight down the fall line to escape an avalanche. You were anxious because you were setting yourself a task that was too much for you at this time. You have protected yourself from what Laurence Morehouse calls the "catastrophe of overeffort." Now that you are no longer demanding the impossible or improbable of yourself, you may even find that you are relaxed enough so that those turns begin to link themselves.

Some people have suggested minimizing fear by calling it something else—"excitement," for instance. Words do have power; it may be that you are psyching yourself out by saying you are "afraid" when you are only hyped up. But generally, we do not think it is useful or even wise to deny fear by slipcovering it. Repackaging the product does not change the ingredients: disruption of muscle control, frustration, impaired judgement, inability to concentrate on the matter at hand. It also denies the positive effects of those feelings, the opportunity to psych yourself up or reevaluate your challenge thresholds. Far better to call fear or anxiety by their proper names and learn to gain control of their effects or use the surge of adrenaline they bring with them.

On the subject of winter driving, Denise McCluggage once wrote that one of the reasons for winter accidents is that drivers do not lose control of their cars, they "give up" control. As the car goes into a spin on a patch of ice, they literally take their hands off the wheel and let the car go instead of fighting to keep it on the road.

The same thing happens when we get in trouble with our skiing. If we hit a patch of ice and start skidding into a fall, we often just let ourselves go into that fall instead of using the shot of adrenaline to steer off the ice or push our edges harder to make them grab.

We all know how we push the button on fear by anticipating disaster. Watch the covey of skiers gathered at the top of a steep pitch. They cluster to the side of the slope chattering, at least mentally, about the calamities that will happen, worrying about the steepness, working themselves up. If they generate what Morehouse calls a state of "optimal anxiety," if they prime themselves with just enough adrenaline and muscular tension to feel alert and powerful, they will ski the slope successfully. If they linger too long, they will work themselves into a state of anxiety that will virtually insure disaster. They will psych themselves out.

But you don't want to abandon responsibility for assessing the risk by simply plunging over the top of the slope. You do want to evaluate the slope and your own feelings, to know whether you will be risking life or limb or merely risking your dignity.

You want to put fear in its proper place.

12

Competition: Winning Isn't Everything but Racing Is Something

Because we have stressed that for women who ski winning isn't everything, it isn't even very much, it is going to be assumed that we think competition—as in ski racing—is bad. Not so. Ski racing is fun.

Competition is bad if it is divisive, if it is frightening, if it is damaging to the racer. Competition is good if it makes the racer—or the runner or the outfielder—stronger. It can be an opportunity to grow, for competitors to push each other to new limits, to spur each other to greater accomplishments.

What is bad about competition is what it has become. Entertainment, spectacle, gladiatorial combat. Ski racing as a sport is not as bad as some, but only, it must sadly be said, because the rewards are not as great as for other sports, and the arena is limited to the number of people who will stand in the cold and watch. If the Nielsen rating on TV skiing even begins to climb, watch out. The recruiters, with checkbooks in hand, will be scouring the rope tows as the basketball scouts now cruise the urban street courts.

As women enter more and more into athletics, they

195

have an opportunity to change that, to turn it around and give competitive games a new focus, an opportunity for talented athletes to stretch their skills and provide joyous models for us all.

Women may shy away from competitive athletics for a number of reasons: fear of failure, fear of success, fear of not pleasing family or friends, fear of making fools of themselves. Because our view of competition has become distorted by the emphasis on winning and on the athlete as performer, competition takes on more importance as proof of worth than it deserves. It can be as satisfying for a racer to finish the course, if that is her goal, as it is to win the race.

Women who are temperamentally competitive, as some of us are, may tend to subdue if not totally deny those feelings. It is not part of the old-fashioned woman's image to "want to beat the hell out of someone else on a race course," as one former racer described it. Competing fiercely or determinedly besting another woman is often considered "mean" or antisocial.

No doubt other more subtle factors also influence a woman's willingness to race, including the wish not to appear "masculine."

On tests of sex differences in personality, top women athletes do show up as more "autonomous" and "independent" than other women. Autonomous and independent are not synonymous with hair on the chest, but Dr. Bruce Ogilvie says in *The Female Runner*, "To succeed [in athletics], a woman has to be able to stand up and spit in the eye of those in charge."

Those same tests indicate that women generally tend to be more social and more sensitive than men. Women like both to seek support and give support to others; they are more tuned in to other people's needs and motives, desires and frustrations.

It is pretty hard to tune in to someone's needs, desires, and frustrations when you're spitting in their eye. By these criteria, it's self-cancelling to be a woman and a winner.

No wonder many women are in conflict about competition. Racing to win is completely incompatible with their roles as women as they perceive them. Women athletes may punish themselves for "unfeminine" behavior by dealing themselves out of the game, or they may, as some do, try to become more masculine than the male.

Many women athletes retain their identity as whole women; they understand that their interest in athletics or competition is only one aspect of who they are. But they must still struggle against the way other people perceive them.

Even today, there are pressures on a woman—on the adolescent especially—to give up competition, to be a "lady," to be "feminine." If those pressures do not come from her family, they may come from her peers or her teachers or simply from the picture she receives through television, newspapers, magazines, and books of what an acceptable role is for a woman. Except for the occasional tennis game or gymnastic event, women on television do not engage in tough competition. Roller derbies are a joke; "Charlie's Angels" never even work up a sweat.

Olympic ski medalist Penny Pitou told the authors of *The Femininity Game:* "A woman once wrote me a fan letter saying what a wonderful young woman she thought I was. She said she hoped my daughter would grow up to be just like me and then added, 'Please don't let the little girl ski.' " The implication was of course, that Pitou was a wonderful woman in spite of her skiing, not because of it.

There are other reasons women evade competition. Many women don't feel comfortable in a testing situation. Giving themselves up to win-or-lose is frightening; it is incompatible with a life role that is still geared to a lack of pressure, a lack of drive, a lack of confrontation.

Some women still fear that competitive athletics will damage their bodies, that they will be unable to bear children or will begin to secrete male hormones and grow a beard, or will stop menstruating. We know now that athletic participation improves a woman's capability to carry and bear children. Women athletes also have far fewer "female complaints," that is, pain or discomfort during menstrual cycles.

It is apparently true that women athletes who overtrain, that is, do too much daily running, jumping, weight lifting, bicycling, do suffer an erratic menstrual cycle; sometimes menstruation even disappears altogether. When the over-training is regulated, when the athlete drops back to a less rigorous schedule or the body adapts to the added stress, menstruation reappears and no damage seems to have been done. Men also suffer from an overtraining syn-drome, but the symptoms are not so dramatic.

Women athletes in good condition do not suffer more injuries than men, as we have pointed out earlier. The injuries may differ in kind because of differences in physiology—looser vs. tighter ligaments, for instance—but not in quantity. What may make it appear that women are more often injured is that (1) women are not in good condition, (2) women's teams do not yet have the expert trainers or qualified physical therapists who are available to men's teams. These specialists help prevent injuries and heal them quickly. Women athletes may also suffer some psychosomatic reactions, symptoms of illness or injury that result not from the athletic performance, but from the conflicts created by social pressures and skewed self-images. It is because of the residue of these stereotypes that many women today shy away from competition or are deterred from it by parents and friends.

As Dr. Kenneth Foreman reported in *The Female Runner*, "The ancient Greeks beheaded any woman who dared watch the warrior athlete perform. In more recent times, females have been psychologically beheaded if they even acted as if they might enjoy vigorous physical activity. . . ."

Actually, the ancient Greeks didn't behead the female spectator, they threw her off a cliff, but women get the message. The Greeks, according to some, were over-reacting to the matriarchal societies which had prevailed in ancient history. It was Aristotle who helped justify the new

trend to patriarchy by describing women as "less coura-
geous, less honest . . . weaker and colder in nature . . . we
must look upon the female character as being a sort of
natural deficiency . . . a misbegotten male."

Thus began the dark ages for women athletes, effectively wiping out the memory of a long line of strong and
active women.

Women can and should take pride in their athletic
history beginning with the Amazons, who have gotten a
bad press since the days of Aristotle. They were not
apparently the vicious, hostile, self-mutilating clan that
legend has them, but a tribe of intelligent, healthy, hard-
working women whose members included the Queen
Penthesileia, described as "divinely tall and most divinely
fair." History includes women of Sparta who trained by
running, jumping, lifting weights, and wrestling, and
the female bull dancers of Crete. But after Aristotle,
athletic women didn't really surface again until the beginning of the twentieth century. In 1900 women were al-
lowed to dip their toes into the modern Olympics with
tennis. Slowly women began to make their way in tennis,
swimming, track and field, golf. Babe Didrikson became a
heroine in both track and golf. So did Suzanne Langlen and
Little Mo Connelly in tennis.

It is also to the unheralded skiers that American women
can look with great pride. In 1935, Alice Damrosch Kaier
(herself a pioneer mountain climber and skier) put together
with her own money a team of American women ski racers
which she entered in the 1936 Olympics in Germany. The
team was dubbed "The Red Legs" (yes, they wore red
stockings) and went on to win nothing. That they existed
at all—unsubsidized, unpublicized, virtually unknown—
was a phenomenon. The first men's team wasn't even
organized until 1948.

Maybe it was this early bonding that helped lead
American women racers to stunningly surpass their coun-
trymen in Olympic and World Championship compe-
titions. Since 1948, when Gretchen Fraser won a gold

and silver in the Winter Olympics, American women have brought home nineteen Olympic and FIS medals for Alpine skiing, including four golds. American men have brought home three. The list of ski champions includes not only Gretchen Fraser and Andrea Mead Lawrence and Penny Pitou, but Janette Burr, Sally Deaver, Betsy Snite, Jean Saubert, Barbara Ferries, Joan Hannah, Penny McCoy, Barbara Cochran, Marilyn Cochran, Susan Corrock, and Cindy Nelson.

This is not to abuse our skiing brothers. But there is something very screwy in a system that has not made these women household words (or at least base-lodge words), whereas the men, Bill Kidd and Jim Heuga, are known and well rewarded. It is not that aspiring young ski racers have no heroines to emulate; it is that they have never heard of the heroines. With the exceptions of Lawrence, the Cochrans, and Cindy Nelson (who is still racing), these Olympic champions have disappeared into the world of kitchens and nurseries or low-visibility ski employment.

We need not feel sorry for those champions—or at least not all of them. Many of them tell us they have willingly turned away from ski racing and the possible rewards of their victories to build full and rich lives for themselves, using what they learned from competition to do so. We can feel sad that they left behind them no record of what it was they learned and what competition did to make them stronger, better women. They have broken the trail, but perhaps through no fault of their own, left no signposts for the rest of us.

And you wonder if the owners of Mount Purple Majesty had been standing at the finish line with a five-figure contract asking them to be director of skiing, if the kitchen and the babies would have been so appealing. Former ski racers who are male proliferate in the hierarchies of skiing. Are all women racers less ambitious, less competent? That's doubtful. It seems rather that the gold and silver medals mined by women somehow are tarnished by their gender.

Why Accept the Challenge of Racing?

If competitive athletics is "unnatural" to women, if we must overcome so many obstacles to participate, why bother? Surely there are other avenues in which to direct our energy, other perhaps more important barriers to break down.

Many of us don't bother—skiing for recreation is enough. To introduce competition into our skiing lives is to turn it into something we do not wish it to be. As many of us jog a mile or two a few times a week, play occasional tennis without any desire to enter a marathon or a tournament, so we ski to enjoy the winter, the outdoors, our pleasure in our own competence, with no desire to race.

For others of us, as ski racer Kiki Cutter says, "Racing keeps skiing interesting." A slalom course is a ready-made goal: to stay on course, to better our own time, to better our neighbor's time. Freestyling expands the options. A spread eagle or a 360 is a clear challenge to our own developing skills. Besides it's fun to do.

There is joy in successful competition because it reinforces our notion of competence and helps us define our potential. It tells us "I can do it." There is great satisfaction in skiing up to your potential and trying on a slalom course for size or perfecting a ballet maneuver.

We hear often how much men benefit from competitive athletics in school. Competitive athletics teaches a boy: to interact with both teammates and opponents, to share in give-and-take, to find self-expression, to develop leadership, to feel accomplishment in completing a task, to test one's limits, to win against odds, to take pride in achieving a personal goal, to lose gracefully. "Learning to give and take in a competitive situation and learning that losing isn't the end of the world can help a girl cope with many other situations that otherwise would be very frustrating," says Thomas Tutko.

Those arguments smack of protesting too much. Ski racing is fun. It is fun for the racer; it is fun for the spectator; it is fun for the judges and gatekeepers and timers (although when the hill is icy and the wind is blowing it's not so much fun). That should be sufficient justification. But if we must add weight to our frivolities, then maybe ski racing does help a girl cope.

There are other benefits. If you race well, you feel good. There is "great satisfaction in developing one's skills to the maximum," says Tutko, no matter if it is a World Cup race or a local Spring Fling.

If it is not fun and does not make you feel good, then there really isn't much point in racing.

One Woman's Way student who had never even considered making a turn around a slalom pole ran a NASTAR (National Standard Races) slalom course at the end of her ski week. She didn't know it was a NASTAR course and that she was being timed or she might not have done it. She loved it, continued racing, and was invited to the NASTAR nationals in Colorado.

Another Woman's Way student, apparently under pressure from family or friends, wanted to ski faster and more aggressively. She wrote later to say that her friends at home told her she was skiing "faster and more aggressively." She promised them she was going to start racing soon.

"I keep telling them that so I'll psych myself into it," she added.

That sounded as if she was still skiing to satisfy someone else's image of her, as if she really had no interest of her own in racing.

"Everyone is not competitive," says Tutko. "Everyone does not like to play to win. Many want to play simply to play."

Even among women who compete, many feel that it is the joy of playing, the thrill of the involvement, rather than the winning, which is rewarding.

To watch Dinah's daughter and her friend Samantha play "Scrabble" is to understand that. They not only make up words from the letters that they have drawn, but they happily trade letters to complete some of their imaginative words. When the question of rules or who won is raised, they dismiss the questioner. All of that is irrelevant to their pleasure in the play.

It is perhaps some of that attitude women can restore to competition. Because women unlike men are still not patterned early on for "success," to compete for money, jobs, status, and recognition, they still compete for pleasure and because they want to. Nor is their sexual identity bound to athletic prowess; they do not have to prove virility by being first through the finish gate.

Women find great reward, studies show, in the bonds that develop among teammates. Their attitude is similar to that of the Chinese: "We feel that the final score of a game is a matter of interest for a few moments, while the friendships developed go on for years, many years," said a Chinese spokesman to a *Sports Illustrated* reporter.

The group of women who gather to compete in a women's professional ski race are examples. Their pleasure at seeing each other, at once again being in a situation where they "play" together is so evident that the races themselves seem almost secondary. On the hill they race to win, sometimes head to head against their best friends (as men do also). But when the women race their companions on the course seem to serve as pacesetters rather than the enemy. They spur each other on to greater enthusiasm and effort. They are determined to win, but not compelled to win.

The solidarity of the women pros as a group is evident, and the subtleties of the differences in attitude is confusing to the media who are trying to produce the routine reports. The racers do not give the same responses as their male counterparts. The winners resist deification, they resist setting up an opponent as "the one to beat," they resist personal rivalries. They express simple pleasure at the opportunity to race, they do not take their roles as winners very seriously, although they take their racing seriously.

It is a difference that observers find hard to absorb, so they do not take women's racing seriously. That attitude is in conflict with the new vision of women as vital, healthy, sports- or activity-oriented human beings which is bandied about in magazines and books. But that is a trap that women should be wary of. As voluptuosness was the standard of female appeal at the turn of the century, languorousness in the thirties and competence in the fifties, so athleticism may be the new sex appeal of these decades. It is one thing to buy a pair of jogging shorts and jog a little or a pair of ski boots and ski a little. It is another to devote the time, energy, money, and inconvenience to ski racing. The ski racer runs smack against all the old stereotypes and myths which she thought were dissolved in the wave of Title IX and the women's movement. There is still discrimination against women athletes in terms of prestige, money, training facilities, sensitive coaches, and opportunities to race. Things are better than they used to be and apparently they're going to continue to improve.

Getting into Racing

How do you become a ski racer? If you're old enough to read this book, it's probably too late to aim for the United States Ski Team.

Ski racers serious about a spot on the national team have been racing since their legs were too short to reach the ground from a chair lift. But if you're past puberty and don't have a wall lined with trophies, don't despair. Both men and women have suffered from the notion that if you're old enough to drive, you're too old to get into ski racing. Coaches and trainers and other athletic gurus are coming around to the belief that, as Janice Kaplan reported in *The New York Times*, "Women, like men, get stronger as they get older." That doesn't mean that we can leap into the starting gate with twelve-year-olds, but it does mean if we're over thirty, we can still try racing if we want to. There is, for instance a very active veterans or senior race program run through the United States Ski Association which begins with club races and culminates in a national championship. You must be over 28 years old to join.

If you're interested in Alpine or x-c competition for yourself or your daughters, the way can begin through club races and programs sponsored by a ski area. Girls can start racing officially as young as six years old, although most wait until they are eight.

Clubs often sponsor races at local hills or at the hill where members ski most frequently.

Seniors now can sign up for spring and summer race camps at western areas where the snow lingers. They are heavily attended.

Many ski schools run youngsters' racing programs on the theory that it keeps them interested, develops talent and keeps the hotdoggers off the hills where recreational skiers are not happy about being blitzed by an adolescent streak, however talented. Enough adults have expressed interest that many areas also have racing classes for them.

Because ski racing is becoming highly sophisticated and the racers who compete—like athletes in all sports—more and more skilled, there are programs that combine school and skiing. These enable youngsters to spend the winter at a ski area where study programs are integrated with ski-racing schedules. Some of the ski areas offer full four-year high school courses and even post-high school, precollege studies. Most of them are either certified by the state as proper educational institutions or work closely with the home school to cover courses and material necessary for a high school diploma.

More and more colleges are offering ski scholarships for women, with the big ski universities gradually upping the ante to attract talented women racers as the women's collegiate program becomes more of an equal opportunity. The schools include the universities of Colorado, New Hampshire, Maine, Utah, Alaska, New Mexico, and Wyoming.

Other schools in snow country may have at least partial ski scholarships available. This is thanks not only to the legislated equality of Title IX but to the loosening of the NCAA and AIAW rules on what constitutes a ski team. The AIAW is the Association of Intercollegiate Athletics for Women, which governs intercollegiate sport for women, as the NCAA does for men.

For women interested in trying freestyle—ballet skiing, mogul skiing—many ski areas offer classes to students of all ages to teach the fundamental techniques. (Most will not teach aerial maneuvers because the chances of injury and the insurance problems are too great.) As skiers advance in their skills, there are training camps scattered around the country which work with advanced freestylers. There is an amateur and a professional freestyle circuit.

Professional racing draws from the ranks of world class or would-be world class amateur racers. Some skiers prefer pro racing because it does not demand the discipline to a system that being a member of a national team does. Of course, it's not subsidized either, so the Alpine or freestyle pro racer must scratch around on her own for sponsors (easier for men than for women) and must discipline herself to training if she wants to win.

NASTAR, the National Standard Races, are immensely popular. For a minimum fee, a woman can race against time set by a national pacesetter. The NASTAR races are fun and challenging because you can measure your progress from week to week. The system is made possible by a complicated manipulation of percentages which only a computer could love. You don't have to figure them. You just race and pick up your times or your gold, silver, or bronze star at the finish line. Women get addicted to running NASTAR courses.

Competition is one aspect of skiing, one role we can play if we choose. If we do not choose to play that role, it is at least important that we come to view women racers as whole people, that we do not see them either as highly trained machines or fall into the trap of viewing women racers as aberrations of nature, as somehow different in kind from other women, somehow less female. If all goes well, our women ski racers will not only continue to win medals, but will be able—if *they* choose—to stay out front as models of what women can achieve.

13

Realizing Our Potential

It is still common cocktail party chatter that we human beings use only 10 percent of our potential. If we only knew how to exercise our brains and our bodies to their limits—Wonder Woman, watch out. Scientists suggest now that the part of us that is unexercised may be less than we imagine. But we still long to be Renaissance women, to be the artist and the scientist, the humanitarian and the athlete, the cook and the critic all at the same time.

Growth and self-improvement is the goal. We take seminars in how to assert ourselves, courses in business management or eighteenth-century philosophy or ski-better weeks. It is easy to stand back and laugh at ourselves, to mock the lists of self-improvement minicourses in the local paper, to wonder at the diet books, running books, the How-I-became-a-famous-movie-star-but-remain-a-wonderful-person-withal books on the best-seller lists. But we should not forget that these phenomena, however banal they sometimes seem, reflect a continuing impetus toward growth, an apparently very strong urge to push against the limits of what we are and get a glimpse of what we can be.

As we take our M.A. and Ph.D. degrees, our seminars on house plants, our Woman's Way weeks, we realize very quickly that it is no longer possible to be a Renaissance woman. The exponential growth of information, the extraordinary number of possibilities for experience now open to us, the limitations on our time and energy, our responsibilities to others make it clear that we cannot realize everything that is possible in us—we cannot be both Julia Child and Jane Fonda. Only the extraordinary among us may even strive to be the complete nurturing mother; the intelligent, directive, foresighted executive; the talented, creative, sensitive artist; the skilled, strong athlete all in the same life.

In skiing, the same principle applies. You can be Cindy Nelson or Suzy Chaffee if you, as they did, through a combination of chance, choice, and talent, order your life so that the bulk of your time and energy is devoted to skiing, to developing the physical resources, concentration, and discipline required.

But for most of us skiing is not the first priority. Despite the benefits we have talked about that skiing can bring to women—self-confidence, self-realization, the recognition of the value of the feminine in the sport—most of us do not choose to devote our lives to skiing.

We put skiing on our A list or our B list or our C list as the life goal experts dictate and put as much time and energy into it as we decide to permit ourselves.

However, as we do that, we should keep in mind what sports in general and skiing in particular can do in helping fulfill our other priorities and our potential. If skiing is somewhere at the bottom of the C list as something that you want to do when you have the odd weekend and a bit of extra money, that's fine. But even on that odd weekend, skiing can help you exercise your whole self.

Our Potential as Human Beings ══════════

One Woman's Way student returns as often as possible to take another seminar. She is excited not only by the changes in her skiing, but by the changes in other aspects of her life. She is, she says, more oriented to the present and not to the past and future. She is better able to make choices, including seemingly insignificant ones such as between red or blue kitchen curtains which had been fertile ground for procrastination and turmoil for her. She also had a striking insight into her relationship with her husband when she realized for the first time that she was at least as competitive as he.

She was obviously using skiing as a testing ground for problems she had already been struggling with at home. The experience of the seminars and the sport clarified the questions for her and gave her some of the answers.

Although she perhaps gives more credit to the sport than is due, many of the techniques of learning and exploring ourselves which we have discussed in this book can be transferred to the rest of our lives: the exercises for relaxed concentration, the techniques of nonjudgmental awareness, the role playing of aggressiveness or frivolity, the realization of the "peak experience," those moments when we lose ourselves completely. Once we have experienced these things on the mountain, then they become more possible and useful in our homes, our offices, on our bicycles.

We can learn, for instance, to take the responsibility for our own lives and our own learning. As we practice taking a lesson, letting the teacher help us learn rather than having her "teach" us, we can carry that over to our own lives. We can, for example, let our boss help us do our jobs, rather than let her "boss" us in our jobs.

Our Physical Potential ━━━━━━━━━━━━━

We can realize the potential of our bodies and the way healthy bodies can help us lead fuller and richer lives.

As the writers of *Our Bodies, Ourselves* point out, "We have in the past accepted limitations on what our bodies can do. We have this notion that mind and body are separate—but how can you feel good in the head, really, if your body's like a limp rag?"

Bodies that are more than limp rags, that have attention paid to them, affect the quality of our lives. Healthy bodies make us feel good, give us more energy, raise our sense of competence, our sense of independence and autonomy, and make us look better. To expand the potential of our bodies adds resources we can use to expand the potential of our minds and spirits.

Yoga exercises are the best way to begin for women who have never paid attention to fitness before. The Woman's Way seminars start every skiing day with a series of Yoga-based stretching exercises—a gentle way of easing into the day and letting your muscles know that you are up and about and interested in their condition. Yoga is where "body awareness" got its start. Not only are Yoga exercises generally good for starting the day, they are specifically good for skiing. Skiing demands flexibility in the muscles and Yoga helps tune up those muscles.

Skiing also demands strength, particularly in the thigh muscles, abdomen, and lower back, and this comes from strength-building exercises: weight machines, bicycling, skiing itself, or your garden variety calisthenics. Hard skiing also demands endurance, the buildup of aerobic capacity through efforts like running or cross-country skiing or jumping rope or lots of Alpine skiing.

You as a would-be better skier can expend some or all or none of the effort necessary to improve your flexibility, strength, and endurance. That, too, is your choice. But when you make the choice, you should understand that if you choose to do none of the above, the opportunity to realize the potential of your body will be diminished. Getting in shape for skiing is work; if you do not work, your ability to master the skills, explore the opportunities of the sport, enjoy its rewards will be that much less. Let us not kid ourselves that if we concentrate and center and suspend judgment of ourselves, we will automatically become good athletes, that our bodies will suddenly become lithe and strong because we are more tuned in to them. We may enjoy our bodies more and get far more pleasure out of our skiing, but our bodies will not become lithe and strong unless we work at it.

Our Potential as Women

Women as women have a unique contribution to make to skiing and to the rest of the world. We must work at that too. It is difficult enough for many of us to come to terms with the idea that we are not born to be timid, frail, and unathletic. It is staggering when we discover that no matter how well a woman skis, no matter how beautifully or fast or "aggressively" she moves, she is never, in the general view, going to ski as well as a man. That has nothing to do with reality, with whether she is, in fact, skiing faster or better, but with how we permit ourselves to perceive a woman's performance.

Let's try an experiment:

Men carve tight turns, women carve large turns. Which is better?

Men carve large turns, women carve tight turns. Which is better?

If you felt yourself twitch in discomfort because your reflex was to go with the way men do things, no matter what, you have company—most men and most women in this country and around the world.

The tendency among women, particularly when it relates to the sports experience, is to accept male standards unquestioningly. But when women set out to achieve these male standards, it is a lifelong scramble.

A study reported in *Psychology Today* indicated that both men and women refuse to perceive women as successful, as leaders. A series of photographs showed a group of people seated around a table with one person in the seat at the head of the table. When a man was seated in the head chair, he was unhesitatingly picked out as the leader of the group. When a woman was seated in that chair, she was almost never chosen as the leader unless the group was all female. The people looking at the slides were simply unable to perceive women as leaders.

Man's work is still considered more important, more valuable than the work that women do. As reported in *The Longest War*, as soon as women take over an occupation, it loses status. Men used to be secretaries and typists and the work of a secretary was considered responsible and important. Women took over the occupation of secretary and we all know how "the girls in the office" are viewed. Teaching was a field reserved for men for many years; women took over the teaching profession at the grammar school and elementary school levels and it immediately dropped in status. In the USSR, women are the doctors; doctors are low in the social hierarchy of that country.

Dinah went to a meeting of journalists and people in the ski industry which included a wide-ranging discussion of where skiing was heading. Two themes emerged. Skiing was no longer being whitewashed as a sport as inherently safe as Ping-Pong but was being reinstated as a risk sport, an adventure. The second was that women in skiing should finally be recognized as skiers in their own right, not as adjuncts to husbands, male friends, or mitten holders for their children.

But, said a young male writer, rising to make what he thought was a telling point: How can you reconcile these two points of view? If you want to identify skiing as a risk sport, how can you sell it to women? This was only weeks after two women had died climbing Annapurna, but he had asked the question seriously. In his mind, women were still timid and fearful and probably frail too.

To chip away at this seemingly intransigent attitude, it is more useful to truly appreciate our potential as women and our "womanly" values than to struggle futilely to prove we can meet a male standard of performance.

"Male instructors have always told me, 'Helen, you have to ski more aggressively.' My question is why?" asked a Woman's Way student.

We're glad she asked that question. "Ski more aggressively" is a good example of a male value being overvalued, of women accepting without question the limits and parameters set by men.

Beverly Johnson, the first woman to climb the 3,000-foot wall of Yosemite's El Capitan, did not "attack" the face. Instead, as someone said, "She danced up the mountain." Johnson herself agreed: "Most of the women are dancers and gymnasts when they climb."

"[Women] use elegant solutions rather than the way we sometimes just resort to muscle when there are difficulties. It makes me think the real fun is in using brain power rather than pure strength," added Yosemite ranger John Dill.

Johnson was doing what author Caroline Bird calls "feminizing the job." She was not modeling herself on the male climbers, but bringing to the problem solutions that are peculiarly her own, peculiarly female. She replaced muscle with finesse, accomplished the same goal, and indeed aroused envy for her grace in the heart of at least one man.

Women can bring to sport and to the appreciation of sport a unique frame of reference, a sense of lyricism, poetry, dance, an appreciation of the aesthetic possibilities of the body. They can add to skiing other values traditionally associated with women—expressiveness, empathy, sensitivity, sociability, and a soft pedal on competitiveness.

By not accepting male parameters blindly, women can add an element of spontaneity and play, of innovative games to skiing. They can help make skiing truly free by enjoying what they are doing at the moment they are doing it, by valuing the process and not the product.

Both students and instructors in Woman's Way come to learn that the way women ski, the way they approach skiing and the values they look for and bring to skiing—cooperation, relaxation, fun in learning, delight in progress, tolerance of error, freedom to admit fear—were not only okay, they added an entire new dimension to the sport. As one instructor said, "We can come out of the closet as women."

To tap all of our potential, we also want to avoid closing off our options. If we discover the delight of "feminizing" skiing, we don't want to reject everything that is masculine, to infer that "aggression" is always wrong. If we learn to tune in to our bodies, to speak body language, we also do not want to forget our verbal/analytical vocabulary which may be useful from time to time. We want to be able to move back and forth using all our capabilities.

As more and more women enter sport, however, we have the opportunity to expand the options for other skiers. We can enrich the sport for everyone by giving proper value to these womanly qualities. We can combine the poetry with the prose, the left hand with the right, the feminine with the masculine, the Yin with the Yang, which will make the sport whole.

One gift women can bring is the ability to express feelings—to laugh, to cry, to "dance" with joy, to growl with frustration, to involve themselves emotionally in their sport. It was sad to watch Dallas Cowboy football player Jackie Smith catching a potential touchdown pass in the end zone at Superbowl XIII—and dropping it. What was sad was not his fumble, but the one abrupt jerk of his body which was all he permitted himself in giving vent to what must have been rage, unbearable frustration, humiliation, sorrow, and fear. Surely he must have wanted to scream and beat the earth, to cry, to touch someone who could give him comfort. Perhaps all that came later, but what we saw was one uncontrollable jerk of his body.

"Athletes should be given back their feelings," says George Leonard, and women can help do that. Skiers, hockey players, tennis players, mountain climbers can learn not only to express sorrow at defeat or frustration or pain, but to express joy, delight, or simple pleasure.

A Woman's Way seminar will often find a class of women on the hill laughing out loud, an unrestrained, bubbling up from the gut kind of laugh, pure pleasure. It is the kind of joy that comes from being free of the pressure to perform and being open to the exchange of energy among the sky and the mountain and the other women in the group, being open to every stimulus around you from the texture of the snow to the feeling of speed. It is also the freedom to respond to that stimulation by laughing, dancing, shouting, crying, giggling.

Women also tend to look at athletes as people, not as "performances." As much as it is possible to generalize, women judge achievement in relative terms. We each develop to be the best we can, and the woman who overcomes her fear of ice has accomplished no less than the freestyler who overcomes her fear of doing a flip. To realize our potential does not necessarily mean that we are all alike, all have the same potential.

Such a view leaves the mountain open to all of us to be the best we can and that includes the talented athlete as well. It would be a loss to everyone to suggest that the superb skier—the skier who wins races or graces a mountain with her style—should not strive to achieve the best she can. It can bring as much pleasure as a piece of music or a beautiful painting to watch a beautiful skier or gymnast or runner do what she does best. Heroines and role models in skiing are in short supply. We should encourage and applaud the gifted ones.

But to appreciate that achievement in personal terms, to understand that athletic performance is but one aspect of the whole person is to take the onus off the athlete to be a god and by implication for us to strive always to be godlike.

To ease or eliminate the competitive stress is a contribution that women can make to sport which cannot be emphasized too much. Fierce competition is contagious; studies have shown that even one person who skis only to win or to be best will infect a whole group with the competitive spirit.

Women athletes do "exhibit a greater tendency to be nuturant. . . . It is as if each team member is being looked after by the others. There is thus greater responsiveness to teammates," according to research reported on by Thomas Tutko and Patsy Neal.

The bond among women can be deep, very deep, transcending even such traditional support as taking care of one another's children or providing a sympathetic ear for tales of disastrous love. This opening up among women happens frequently in Woman's Way ski classes. The women are there to have a good time, to learn to ski better, to vacation. They are not there to explore their psyches or raise consciousness. But in the process of spending a happy week together, a deeper connection is tapped.

One beginner reported, "I accomplished something wonderful today. I went up a lift and I skied down. Now someone else might not think that is wonderful, but I am not very athletic, and for me it is. And you know, everyone in the seminar that I told about it said, 'That's wonderful.' They all cared about my accomplishment."

Often at the end of a Woman's Way seminar, the entire group, which has been divided into classes roughly by ability, will ask for a day to ski all together. They ask because they have come to like each other, because they want to spend as much time together as possible before the group breaks up, because they want to have fun together. Often the differences in ability are great, but the more expert skiers happily go to an easier slope and the less advanced do their best to keep up or join in games or run races that will keep the group together. It is as free and relaxed an atmosphere as we have ever seen on a ski slope.

It shows what skiing can be—that the simple pleasures of movement and skill, the harmony of mind and body, the creative forces that sport is supposed to nourish, are there for all of us to take. Given this freedom, this opportunity for spontaneous pleasure, we can explore not only who we are as skiers, but who we are as people.

We can realize our potential.